Tents, Tortoises, and Tailgates:
My Life as a Wildlife Biologist

Scott Lillie

Scott Lillie

DEDICATION

To my family that was always there for me, no matter how crazy my job seemed to them.

CONTENTS

Preface:

For many people, Monday morning consists of a commute through the suburbs or the city to work, probably arriving to punch a time card or login on a computer. This is usually followed by time at a desk and mingling with coworkers by the water cooler. Maybe at some point during the week the office goes to lunch or happy hour at the corner restaurant. Afterwards they drive home to a house or an apartment to a waiting wife or husband, maybe a dog or cat. They probably turn on their favorite television shows, relax on a comfortable couch, and eat a home-cooked dinner. If it has been a hard day, they may order a pizza or take-out instead. Then it's off to a nice soft bed, only to repeat it all again until the weekend arrives. It's a stable life. Most might say it's a normal life. However, for some of us this stable and "normal" life is as far from normal as it gets.

For a small group of people, instead of rush hour on the freeway, they are usually up before dawn driving narrow dirt roads—no time card, no computer login. Instead of a brief case, it's a field bag. Instead of dress shoes, it's hiking boots. The gathering spot isn't the water cooler, it's the last drivable spot that a truck can fit in before having to continue on foot or in a kayak. There are no restaurants to eat lunch or dinner at, and the break room is your work truck. After a hard day of work, all you have to look forward to is a primitive camp site, the bed of a pickup truck, or maybe a crowded bunk house. Food is kept in ice chests, not refrigerators. Cooking is done on camp stoves, not the oven. Bed is a sleeping bag, or if you're lucky, a stiff bunk mattress. No TV, no couch, and most of the time, no electricity or running water. At the end of the day, most of these people get paid little more than minimum wage, have no health insurance, and are applying for new jobs and moving to another remote location every three to six months. These people are collectively known as field biologists—not the ones you see making the rounds on morning talk shows, or the "wildlife experts" you might see on bad reality TV, but the ground-level people conducting surveys, gathering the data, and restoring habitats, the people making a real difference in conservation. It would be safe to assume anyone that chooses to belong to this group is either dedicated or crazy. I am one of these people, and I have not decided which one of those terms describes me, yet.

Field biologist sounds like a romantic job, a job people often think how lucky one must be to have. At times, it is exactly what people think: seeing amazing and remote places, holding cute and fuzzy animals, and trying to save the environment. But those moments are the rewards after hours of grueling work and surviving some of the harshest environmental conditions nature can throw at you, not to mention making many social sacrifices, as well. Some people do it their whole lives, others only a few years. The lucky ones may eventually settle down with a government agency job. I have been working as a field biologist for nearly ten years. This is my story, from face to face encounters with rattlesnakes and mountain lions in the burning deserts of the Southwest, to dealing with snow, ice, and tornados in the Midwest. From alligators and cottonmouths in southern swamps, to sharks, sea turtles, and beaches in the Caribbean, and from tents and cots, to hotels and luxury vacation homes. These are the stories from my travels. This is my life as a field biologist.

Introduction:

It had been a week now since I had left training and started surveying for the elusive southwestern willow flycatcher, and by this time I was really getting into the flow of things. I rarely went off my bearing now, this after an earlier incident of wandering nearly 50 feet off my survey line, which ended with me reporting my crew lead's survey tape as a new bird. Since then, things had been going well—until the day I had an incredible animal encounter that I will never forget.

We were surveying in smaller groups and I was on the edge of the survey line. I was walking as normal, playing my bird call every 30 feet or so, when I heard something return the call. Not the quiet "fitz-bew" I was used to hearing, but more of a shrieking, eerie "CAK! CAK! CAK!" from above. Looking up, I was just in time to see a Cooper's hawk swooping down straight at my face! I let out my own alarm call and dropped to the ground. The hawk pulled up about three feet from my face and took to the air again. To say I didn't curse at the hawk would be a lie. In fact, I called it every name I could think of, mostly because of how foolish I felt dropping to the ground.

I rose up caked in mud and started my transect again, thinking how strange the encounter was. After walking about another 20 feet I heard the hawk calling again and looked up. Again, the hawk streaked down at my face! Despite my best efforts, I went to the ground again. Seeing a large hawk with huge talons flying 30 mph at your face will make most people drop. It pulled up only two feet away this time. At this point, I realized I wasn't imagining it—this hawk was attacking me! Of all the dangers in the desert I came prepared for I never thought of an aerial assault. I turned to the right and started to jog, just wanting to get out of the area. Going to the right was apparently the wrong choice, as the shrieking calls rang out closer together now. The hawk made another run, this time pulling up just a foot from my face. Again, I cursed. I was in panic mode now. I went full speed straight ahead, crashing through the brush, swearing the whole time. I finally crashed through some rather thick brush and skidded to a halt, right in front of my very-surprised crew leader.

When I told her the whole story she did her best not to laugh. Did her best, but did not succeed. I was covered in sweat and mud. I had a few tree branches attached to various parts of my clothing and I had lost my hat at some point during the run. I was disheveled to say the least.

I vaguely remembered reading something in college that some hawks will defend their nest from large predators—I guess now I knew how they did it. I later found out that the Cooper's hawk did indeed have a nest in the area. When I made my turn to leave I actually headed straight towards the nest and further enraged the hawk. Looking back, seeing a hawk from a foot away in the wild was amazing. Seeing it protect its nest from a predator was even more amazing. However, seeing it from a safe distance a little later was probably my favorite view. During the year, I continued to visit the nest (from a safe distance) and watched the chicks grow up and eventually fledge. After that incident, I came away with an even greater respect for birds of prey, and went on to complete my first summer in the field.

***

That experience from my first summer as a field biologist was even more remarkable considering I had been living in the 7th largest city in the United States, and attending one of the largest universities in the country just a few months prior. So how did I become a field biologist? To be completely honest I never thought of myself as an outdoors person while growing up. My family would camp and fish once or twice a year like a lot of families do. We would go up to a small town in northern Arizona called Greer, a great place with streams, lakes, and pine forests. It was small, having only one gas station and one general store. Even though I still felt like a city kid out of place, I did enjoy being up there. I looked forward to going there each summer, but to me it was just a fun summer trip. It wasn't a lifestyle or a passion, at least not yet. It certainly wasn't a career. I definitely never expected to end up in the heart of the Sonoran Desert, camping out for ten days at a time, and looking for endangered birds during one of the hottest summers I could remember.

As I got older, I developed an interest in wildlife and the environment, and after starting college I thought I would end up as a park ranger working just outside Phoenix, or maybe at the Phoenix Zoo. After several odd jobs that included working at Subway, a call center, the college library, and loading trucks at a warehouse, the summer before my senior year I was offered an internship with the Arizona Game and Fish Department (AZGFD). I was very excited when I received the offer, but that did not last long. Instead of working with cool, exciting animals, I was tasked with teaching boating safety to children—ironic because I had never been in anything other than a canoe before. I spent the first half of the summer teaching straight from the book I was given, all the while trying to learn about boating myself. I spent the second half of the summer learning to waterski and wakeboard on my lunch breaks and after work. It certainly wasn't a horrible way to spend the summer, but in no way did it prepare me for the career or life that was in front of me. It did not prepare me for the weeks spent camping, the absolutely brutal competition for permanent positions, or the years I would spend wandering the backcountry doing seasonal work. No, that all came as a surprise. However, what this internship did do was introduce me to AZGFD, and get me started me on the path I walk today.

After a little more than four years and a summer internship, I finally graduated from Arizona State University ready for my career as a wildlife biologist, and my family came together to celebrate. All of my siblings had already graduated and started successful careers. One of my sisters was a lawyer for the State of Arizona. My other sister was the volunteer coordinator for one of the suburbs surrounding Phoenix, while my brother was making big money working for a bank as a systems programmer. And then there was me: a wildlife biologist hopeful, ready to save the world. Currently, I was a part time "ranger" at a local botanical garden, but that actually was little more than a security guard position. I had no idea where to go from there (thanks, ASU). It turned out that my parents almost foreshadowed my travels. For my graduation gift I was given an old-style compass engraved with "Congratulations, love Mom and Dad". A compass…to keep me from getting lost, I guess. I've kept that compass with me through the years and it has never failed to bring a smile to my face when times were tough.

1 The Willow Flycatcher

"The southwestern willow flycatcher is a subspecies of the willow flycatcher. A member of the *Empidonax* genus of flycatchers and is usually identified by call." This was what I was reading as I sat waiting for my phone to ring. I was waiting for my first phone interview. A few weeks earlier I had applied to every job I saw on the Arizona Game and Fish Department website, along with any other jobs I found with wildlife organizations, zoos, or aquariums located in Arizona. The one job that had called me back was a position as a wildlife technician. I would be surveying and nest monitoring for the federally-threatened southwestern willow flycatcher.

My career choice was very foreign to my parents. I still remember their response when I told them of my interview: "Is that a bug?" That was their first response—a bug! Of course it wasn't a bug, but before I replied I looked it up in my bird guide, just to be certain. No it was not a bug, it was a bird.

When it all was said and done, it was my internship with AZGFD that had landed me the job. That and two amazing crew leaders that took a chance on me. And so that was how it all began, my new life as a field biologist.

***

It was May, and I was heading out for my first 10-day camping session. The first five days consisted of training, followed by five days of surveying. I was excited and nervous when I pulled my car into the area that was to be my home for the next five days. The San Pedro River looked like something out of a movie—it was a riparian area full of cottonwood and willow trees, and I could hear the babble of the creek and various birds calling. The camp site was a cleared grassy field with a small cabin on top of a hill. Everything about the place seemed exactly what I had hoped for.

Training soon started, but this wasn't the typical office training that consisted of filling out paperwork or learning how to use the printer. We jumped right into compass use, taking bearings, and estimating distances from objects. When in the field—the term biologists use for when we are out of the office working or camping—you cannot simply carry a tape measure to a nesting bird site. If you do, you run the risk of the bird abandoning that nest and having it wasting valuable time and energy during breeding season. Worse, you could force the young birds out of the nest too early, before they can fly. So for the first few days of training, we practiced estimating distances to trash cans, cars, branches, and rocks, and then measuring the actual distance. I got bored pretty quick, but the training was essential, and I managed to get through it. The next day we started on survey techniques. Surveys for song birds are often done by using call playback during the start of breeding season. The migrant birds fly to an area and try to set up territories; the older the bird, the bigger the territory. The call we played simulates a challenging male. If another male is in the area it will call back to defend its territory. So we would line up and walk a straight line following a compass bearing while playing our tape every 30 feet until we were out of suitable habitat. Sometimes it was only a few meters, sometimes we would be crashing through brush for over a kilometer. We ended training hiking along the San Pedro River playing the famous call of the flycatcher: "fitzbew!"

***

Fitzbew! That's a sound I will never forget. I heard it played every minute or so for a month of surveys. It's a very distinct bird call, as well as a call that helped create such lasting memories.

After training ended, we moved from the paradise of the San Pedro River to Roosevelt Lake in central Arizona to start our surveys. For the first few days of surveys I was put on the Salt River side of the project. The other side was called the Tonto side due to the Tonto Creek inflow. The Salt River side was heavily invaded by an Asian tree species called tamarisk, also known as salt cedar. Salt cedar grows incredibly thick and provides little to no habitat for any species other than birds and invertebrates. It was originally brought to the Southwest as a form of erosion control after all the native willows and cottonwood trees had been cut down along streams and rivers.

The whole reason for surveys and monitoring was due to the water level of the lake being raised several feet in an effort to create a better water reservoir system for central Arizona. We were there looking at how this fluctuation in water level affected the nesting habits of the southwestern willow flycatcher. It was the former inundation of the habitat that created such a horrible survey environment. All the dead trees and branches and all manner of trash had been pushed up against the still living trees, creating six-foot-high walls of brush. These walls were nearly impenetrable, and we had to crawl through a maze of thorny, poking brush while trying to stay on a bearing and walking a straight line. This was nothing like the open banks of cottonwoods and willows I saw at the San Pedro River. No, this was a tamarisk-filled nightmare.

On the second day of surveys on the Salt River I had a great surprise. I was walking on a straight-east bearing when I came to yet another wall of dead brush. This wall went on for several hundred feet in either direction. Trying to walk around it and get back into my original position was out of the question, since I would surely miss my mark. I started to inspect the wall and found a small rabbit-sized opening. The humidity and cooler temperatures in the thick of the brush had kept the ground moist and slightly muddy—lucky me. And so, with a sigh, I decided to take my chances crawling through a hole not much wider than my shoulders.

I had given up trying to not get scratched an hour into the

first day of surveys. After what seemed like hours of crawling (though it was probably only a few minutes) I saw the end of the tunnel. Good timing, too, because my claustrophobia was beginning to kick in. So, with my arms pinned at my side I shimmied my way toward the light. Just as I was about to emerge and get out of the poking, muddy nightmare, I heard a sound most people dread to hear: a buzzing, a rattle.

Stretched out and laying in the sun at the entrance to the brush tunnel was a three-foot-long western diamondback rattlesnake, a very common snake in the desert southwest. With its rugged scales and a camouflaged diamond pattern, I probably would have crawled right over it if it had not sounded off. I was now eye to eye with it, and it had sprung up into a defensive posture. "Great," I thought, "now he is definitely not moving." I was right—it stood its ground watching me. In no position to try to wrangle the rattlesnake, I had two options: wait it out or turn back. At this point, I was done with the tunnel, so I chose the second option and started backing my way out. As fun as it was going forward through that thorny mess, it was even better going backwards in it.

I eventually ended up back where I started. I was new to my job, so I did not really appreciate how amazing it was having a close encounter with such an iconic snake. They truly are amazing creatures, and it added a good memory to an otherwise rough day.

***

During the summer, one of the more desired jobs was the kayak surveys. There were some parts of the lake that still flowed well into the forested areas, and while the tamarisk could not survive being inundated with water, the native willows and cottonwoods could. The idea of gently floating on the lake listening for birds sounded amazing, but there turned out to be a catch.

After quickly volunteering for kayak surveys, we went to the lake to do a quick demonstration on how to launch and control the kayak. I should have known it was coming. As soon as we arrived the crew leader asked me to give a quick lesson on the kayaks since I had spent the last summer as a boating safety instructor for the department. Great. During my interview, I may have embellished a bit on my kayaking skills, which at that point were non-existent. We had used motor boats during my summer as an instructor. I tried my best to remember everything the book had taught me. I drug my kayak to the water and assumed the correct position and shoved into the water. Success! I swung my head around to address my students and that's when I lost my balance. The kayak swayed once to the right, I over corrected and SPLASH! Into the water I went. Lesson over. The crew leads took over after that. At least there wasn't mud this time.

Shortly after my training incident we finally embarked on the kayak surveys. Because the logistics of trying to organize survey lines in kayaks was too difficult, we ended up surveying alone most of the time. After what seemed like hours of paddling, I finally made it to my site.

Kayaking is harder than it looks. Again, my expectations were not the same as the reality. My site was filled with dead trees half underwater. Everywhere I looked the dead trees expanded for what seemed like miles. Paddling was no longer an option, and so I simply pulled my kayak along using the dead trees.

After paddling a few feet into the dead forest I felt something hit my face: sticky threads of a spider web. I turned the kayak slightly to get a view looking into the sunrise, and my stomach dropped. When the first rays of the sun hit the dead trees, thousands of large spider webs began to shine in the sun. Every tree was connected by them. It reminded me of something out of a horror movie. There was no going around them. I knew I could not call off my surveys because of spiders. If I did, I might as well just pack up my tent, go home, and throw away my diploma because my career as a biologist would be over. Time to grow up. I swallowed my fear and started in.

At first, I was using my paddle to cut through the webs, but after almost tipping over twice I just started using my hands—no need to endanger the $1000 pair of binoculars they gave me to avoid spider webs. After making pretty good progress in the forest I felt something crawling on my head. I lost it. I flailed madly. I made contact with one of my frantic blows. It was a spider, a large brown spider. It hit the water of the lake and—to my horror—the spider stayed afloat. It could run on the water due to the surface tension, and came right back to my kayak. At this point, I stopped looking for birds and looked at my kayak. This was another bad choice. I saw three more large spiders on the front of my kayak, then another climbing on the side. I feel like I handled myself heroically until I felt the ones on my legs. I immediately leaned over to reach into the kayak and hit the spider on my leg. The shift in weight made my kayak lurch sharply to the right, and just like in training, I over corrected, and into the water I went.

Now I was floating in water holding my $1000 pair of binoculars over my head in one hand and holding onto the kayak with the other. I looked around. No shore in site. I knew the closest shore was through the spider forest. I knew it, but it didn't mean I had to like it. I was about to start swimming that direction when out of pure chance I saw a large black object floating next to me. It was my wallet. Apparently Velcro may do wonders in space, but isn't so great underwater. Luckily, I had noticed it before swimming away.

It was almost a quarter of a mile to shore. Have you ever tried swimming a quarter of a mile in hiking boots? Try doing it while dragging a kayak! After finally making it to shore I emptied the water out of the kayak and stripped down to my boxers. I then laid my clothes on top of the kayak to dry (it wouldn't take long since it was the summer). After my experience, I was tired and needed to wait for things to dry out, so I decided to take a break and sit in the shade for a minute.

I ended up nodding off to sleep. I am not proud of that, but I was exhausted from the swim and trying to sleep in a hot, windy campsite. It had only been about 30 minutes, and it would have taken that long for my clothes to dry anyway. Upon walking back to the kayak to retrieve my clothes, I was surprised to find one of the largest western diamondback rattlesnakes I have ever seen stretched out next to my kayak. Most days, I would have loved to see it, but since I had surveys to do and it was essentially guarding my clothes, it was rather inconvenient.

I decided to stomp my feet and try to scare it away. If you ever want to feel ridiculous, try yelling and stomping your feet at a five-foot-long rattlesnake while wearing nothing but your boxers. Needless to say, it did not go away. Instead, it retreated to safety underneath my kayak, which I had flipped upside down to dry out. After a minute, I flipped the kayak and the snake immediately started rattling and backing up to the kayak again. This was shaping up to be similar to the encounter I had the first week.

I was able to retrieve my boots, which had been placed at the base of the kayak. After retrieving my boots, I found a stick to move the snake. Having never even moved a rattlesnake with a snake hook, moving it with just a tree branch proved difficult. Unlike in the movies, the snake did not chase me. In fact, it proved to be rather stubborn about moving at all. After poking at it multiple times I eventually got the branch under the snake, lifted, and before I moved more than a foot the snake flopped off the branch. It immediately put its back to the kayak again. I tried again, got the branch under the snake, and lifted, this time moving the snake two feet before it fell off. I wasted no time and put the branch down in front of it again. After about three more tries and a very tense five minutes, I got the snake away from the kayak.

Eventually, I did end up completing my surveys and did not develop any spider powers along the way. It was, however, a very long morning.

***

While doing field work I have met some very interesting people, and the crew at Roosevelt Lake was no exception. When you work and camp with the same crew for weeks and months on end, it enables everyone to get to know each other a lot faster than coworkers you only see at work. You get to know every little quirk about them, which usually means you either get very close with your crew, or you avoid them like the plague. Luckily, I became close with my crew at Roosevelt Lake.

The other biologists in the willow flycatcher (WIFL) crew were mostly older than me, with the exception of the two interns, and were all at least partly responsible for starting me on my path in wildlife biology.

The crew was pretty diverse in both age and personality. There were two crew leaders, a handful of technicians and two interns. I became close with most of the crew during my time there. Their ages ranged from 21 to 50+. There were hunters and vegans and everything in between.

The first thing I should mention is we camped at the Windy Hill camp site. The site lived up to its name. By the end of the first week my tent had blown down twice. After the second time it went down, I decided to leave it down. I simply laid down on the picnic table and slept there. It was cooler and required less work. Later in the year, I switched to a cot after waking up to a horrible spider bite and finding black widows everywhere underneath the picnic table.

This worked fine until later in the summer when a monsoon storm rolled in. It was a welcome relief at first, but I will admit it was a little unnerving. With monsoon storms usually comes thunder and lightning. Seeing that I was under a metal roof laying in a metal framed cot on a hill, I think my fears were justified. The storms came every night for about a week—lightning, wind, and rain. I never fixed my tent from when the wind knocked it down, so I was in a predicament. One of our rules for the campsite was that since the trailer couldn't fit all of us, no one was allowed to sleep there. Well, I was usually the last one up at night, so after everyone went to bed I would sneak into the trailer and sleep. I would get up a few minutes before everyone else and pretend I just walked to the trailer. The storms eventually passed and I moved back to my exposed cot.

Camp life was hard in the desert but could also be fun at times. Our schedule consisted of getting up an hour before sunrise and working until it was too hot for the birds to call, which was usually between 10 AM and noon. Then we would organize our notes and data. Work was usually done by 1 PM, which gave us about seven hours before sunset. The average temperature at that time was around 110 degrees F. We had one air conditioned trailer but we couldn't all fit in there at once and it only brought the temperature down to 85-90 degrees. Most days, a few of us would take turns playing scrabble in the trailer, or napping in the shade. After scrabble we would all usually converge around dinner time to cook, drink beer, talk about our days, and tell stories.

When I came to the job I had very few stories and adventures, and had barely traveled out of Arizona. During the evenings, when we were all waiting for the temperature to drop so we could sleep, everyone would tell stories of past wildlife jobs, or trips to find amazing wildlife. People talked about seeing the most colorful birds imaginable in South America, seeing wolves and grizzles in the northern states, and seeing snakes and amphibians out east. They would go on and on about adventures they had been on with various crews they worked with. When it came to me, I had virtually nothing. The best stories I had involved kicking out prostitutes from the park I had worked at as a ranger. Sure it was a funny story, but it can only be told so many times. At that point, I was just a young kid fresh out of college, eager to have more adventures so I could make some stories of my own.

***

About halfway through the summer we all went a little crazy—I don't know whether it was from dehydration, the sun frying our brains, or just plain boredom. One night, after a brutally hot day I was up with Blondie—one of the female techs I had gotten close to during the season—drinking a beer. We both had been talking about how there was no way we were getting any sleep in this heat. Then a joke came up about the lake a mile away. Why not go for a swim? And after another beer it was no longer a joke—we started walking. It wasn't until we got there that we realized neither of us brought a swimsuit. Horrible situation, especially for a guy, right? I will admit drinking and then skinny dipping is a horrible combination, and one I would not do again, but I was young, and my brain was fried from the desert, so I obviously wasn't thinking clearly. After cooling off, we laid out towels and sat to talk. I guess the beer, dehydration, and fatigue set in because we both fell asleep on the dock. The next thing I remember was waking up to a few fishermen loading a boat. Thankfully, I was in boxers. Blondie was up and mostly dressed by then. I sat up not knowing what else to say so I asked them if they were having any luck. The fisherman looked at me with a grin and said, "Not as much as you apparently." Smartass. And so we both finished getting dressed and hurried back to camp hoping to escape detection by the rest of the crew.

A week or so after the dock incident, morale for the whole crew was getting low and people were tired of the heat. It was one of the older members of our crew that helped out on this one. He organized a group dinner followed by a beer tasting. He had gone to the store and bought a bunch of six packs of every type of beer they had. This was very nice of him considering how little we were paid. This store in rural Arizona obviously didn't carry a large selection, but it was still fun. We all took a small sample and he would talk to us about the brewer and the type of beer. Fun, but at the same time some of the beers I just wanted to drink. I mean most of us were pretty familiar with Corona (it wasn't exactly new to Arizona). Overall, it was a good night and a good morale-booster. Come to think of it, beer has played a role in a lot of field work team-building over the years.

Besides learning about wildlife that season I had also learned a few other life lessons. When I started out that season I took worse care of myself than most college students. My breakfast was usually a Snickers bar and a Pepsi. Then I would eat sunflower seeds while hiking. My lunch was usually beef jerky and some ice cream I would get at the only gas station in the area. After that, I would have a few beers and eat spaghetti or macaroni and cheese for dinner. Combine that with the lack of sleep and I'm surprised my body didn't give out the first month. It was the crew that was responsible for eventually changing my eating habits. At the end of each 10-day field stint we would have potluck dinners, which are pretty common among field crews. Seeing that a lot of the crew were vegetarians and vegans, they had learned how to cook. Despite not having any meat, the meals they cooked were pretty delicious, not to mention healthy. I always felt bad bringing spaghetti when they had such good food. Eventually I broke down and asked my family and coworkers for recipes. I soon started making stir fry and other real dinners, and was adding more and more vegetables to my meals. By the end of the season I was eating real meals at least three times a week.

When we weren't having potlucks we would sometimes get together and go into Tonto Basin to beat the heat. The nearest town was a tiny place that appeared to be stuck in the 1950s. It even had an old gas station where you still had to write down the amount of gas you pumped on a piece of paper. A calculator was then used to figure out the total. The only restaurant was combined with the bar and general store. It was called "The Butcher Hook." As you might imagine, they were not exactly used to seeing a bunch of young people from outside the area frequent the bar. Knowing that a lot of rural Arizonans don't really like government agencies, we all just pretended to be interns or college students. They generally treated us very well, but I did learn another valuable life lesson there: never enter a pool tournament in a small country town full of retired veterans. You will lose, because that is all they do there, apparently—that and fishing. Despite my loss, it was definitely a memorable place and I would highly suggest paying a visit.

Going to restaurants and playing scrabble wasn't the only thing we did on our down time. Some of us would visit the historic cliff dwellings nearby, while others would occasionally swim in the lake. We also spent some of our downtime looking for wildlife. At night we could simply walk or drive down the roads, and usually at least find a few snakes. One day the intern—who many of us affectionately referred to as the Boy Scout—and I planned a trip to find some big horn sheep, since neither of us had seen one in the area yet. We packed our gear, which consisted of several liters of water and head lamps in case we weren't back by nightfall. We went over maps and gave out our planned route to the crew in case of emergency. After a twenty minute drive, we parked, strapped our gear on, and finally started the hike. Then, after walking no more than two hundred feet from the car we looked up, and posing perfectly on a rocky cliff in front of us was a huge big horn ram. Hours of planning, 30 lb. pack on my back, and the animal is practically hanging out in the parking lot. It was great to find our target species, but a little anticlimactic to say the least. Sometimes it's easy being a biologist. Sometimes...

***

We had passed the midway point of the season and things were winding down. The birds had laid their eggs and now we were observing the young. In order to document what we called "nest success," we would count how many eggs that hatched, and keep track of how many of the young survived. The nest surveys were done for the rest of the season. Most of the job at this point was hiking to the nest and sitting quietly making observations.

One of my favorite nests to visit was on the very edge of our survey area. It was my favorite because on a cliff nearby was a nest not made by flycatchers but a bald eagle nest! I first found out about it after hiking one day and seeing a bald eagle on the side of the river devouring what looked like a catfish. I sat and watched it for quite a while before it left, and after asking around I found out there was a nest site nearby. The eagle had two fledgling chicks and every time I would go to that area I would stop and check on them. To be able to watch the chicks grow up and eventually leave the nest for good was an experience I will never forget.

Amazingly, the bald eagle nest was not my most spectacular encounter during the nest success portion of our surveys. One day, I was surveying a nest in an area where they had increased the amount of water exiting the lake, leaving many of the trails I followed earlier in the season underwater. I was heading to the nest, which was surrounded by extremely thick brush, and the trail I needed was underwater. After thinking about it I dropped my gear and decided to wade through the water the rest of the way, since all I really needed was my notebook and binoculars. The water was waist-deep and flowing well. I finally got to the nest and settled in. Luckily, it was in a clear area within the thick brush surrounding the river.

After about half an hour of watching the nestlings, I was wrapping up my notes when I heard something moving in the brush. I figured it was a skunk. I hated when the skunks came through. One of my worst fears was having to camp for ten days smelling like a skunk. I kept writing, trying to finish up quickly. I heard more movement and caught a shadow out of the corner of my eye. I looked up at a shadow about four feet tall emerging from the river side of the brush. The creature walked into the clearing across from me. My mind was not ready to comprehend what I was seeing: it was a mountain lion. The tail was much longer than I thought it would be. The cat must have just crossed the river because it was dripping wet. It looked even more menacing than I imagined. I froze. At this point, all my training escaped me. I was doing everything you shouldn't be doing in mountain lion habitat: I was quiet, crouched, and not moving. Finally, my brain reacted and I jumped to my feet. The lion was only about 50 feet away from me at this point. It looked at me and froze. Then, in what seemed like two bounds, it was gone. The encounter seemed to last five minutes, but was probably more like 20 seconds.

I will never forget when I locked eyes with that lion—or the walk back after I lost sight of him. Too afraid to go waist-deep in water, I crashed through the brush. I was singing and being as loud as I could. I evaluated my weapons: a pocket knife and my binoculars on a sling that I could use as a makeshift flail. Not good. I eventually made it back to my truck and then back to camp. I told my story to the crew, figuring the whole time that no one would believe me. It was one of the veteran crew members that believed me first. He asked the nest number and replied, "Oh yeah, I saw fresh lion tracks there yesterday." Really!? And you didn't tell me? At least they believed me, and I added yet another amazing experience to my first field season.

One day while nest monitoring I had yet another surprise visit. I was crouched down observing the nest when I heard movement in the vegetation. There was a lot more movement than during my mountain lion encounter, and wild thoughts went through my mind. Was it a bear? A Sonoran Sasquatch? Maybe a heard of javelina? Nope, to my surprise it was one of our interns. My relief was short-lived, as I figured that if she were here it probably wasn't a good thing. I was right.

She quickly explained to me that she had taken a wrong turn, got her truck stuck, and wanted my help digging it out. How could I say no to being the hero? I took her to my truck and we drove back to where she got stuck. After turning down a few sketchy sandy washes, I asked her to let me know when the sand got bad so I could stop before we got stuck. Seconds after asking her I felt the truck sink in the sand. We were stuck. So much for letting me know when. Really, I should have known better, since I was driving. The worst part was I could not even see her truck and we were almost to the lake. She had driven her truck to the edge of the lake. She was so close that the sand was saturated in water! I was impressed at how far she had actually made it. I don't think she could have gotten the truck in a worse position short of driving into the water.

We decided to get my truck unstuck first and go for help. Neither of our cell phones worked and we had no radio. After an hour of digging and gathering branches we had moved my truck less than a 100 feet. This wasn't what alarmed me. What did was that I was down to half a liter of water and it wasn't until then I realized she had not been drinking. When I asked her about that she finally decided to tell me she had forgotten her water and only had coffee to drink since breakfast. It was over 100 degrees out! We had been shoveling for an hour, and I was surprised she was still standing.

I looked around and knew we were only about two miles from a group of houses in the middle of nowhere that we could try for help at. Other than those houses it was just uninhabited desert. Still, two miles with no water and a dehydrated girl was a lot to ask. We ended up risking it. Looking back, I probably should have sat her in the shade with my water and gone for help on my own, but really there was no good decision here.

We made it to the community of about 20 houses in an hour, but by then she was looking bad. Her skin was bright red and she felt dizzy. I knocked on doors of the first few houses, but no answer.

Finally, we just went to a random house and drank straight from the hose. We poured some water over our heads then went back to knocking on doors. Eventually, a very nice older lady let us in to use her phone to call for help. While we waited for someone to come get us she actually cooked some tamales and gave us ice cold Kool-Aid—not a bad reward. It wasn't until I was riding to camp in the crew leader's car that it was brought up that it could have been my appearance that scared the elderly community into not helping us. I was about six feet tall and weighed just under 200 lbs. I was soaking wet from the hose, all my clothes were stained and had holes big enough to fit a fist through, and I was sporting a month-old beard. Why not let a homeless man that wandered in from the desert in your home? Everything eventually worked out. The whole crew went out that night and dug both trucks out. It took about two hours and a lot of manpower. I bought a 12-pack of beer for the crew to split as a thanks.

***

During the last few days of the field season we started to document nest selection. This involved collecting data on where the birds decided to build their nest, and was done to determine if one species of tree, the tree's height, or any other particular aspect of a tree was preferred to the others. These were known as "vegetation plots," or "veg plots" for short. During these veg plots I finally got to help on the Tonto side of the river. After three months of crawling through horrible walls of vegetation, kayaking through the spider forest, and wading through rivers, I got to see what other members of the crew experienced. The Tonto side had scattered cottonwood and willow groves with small streams trickling between them. There were clear beaches next to the river and easy walkways wherever you went. A nice canopy offered shade from the sun and rain. No thorns, no dead vegetation walls. No, this was the type of area where you would have a picnic. I will admit I was bitter. While my field season was fun, it was also one of the hardest summers I have ever had. While I suffered through it, the Tonto crew might as well have skipped during their surveys. I eventually got over it, but not before a few days of bitterness.

***

After documenting nest selection—and with the end of the field season getting closer—came one of the most dreaded jobs for a field biologist: data entry. It's a job in which people that have been camping and working in the wilderness come back to the city and stare at a computer screen for eight hours a day. While returning to the city is usually welcomed for a time, it does take some adjustments. I guess one of the biggest adjustments is clothing. At camp and in the field no one cares what you wear, and I rarely wore clothes without holes in them. Salt stains and ripped clothing are the norm in the desert. Nothing really matches, and using duct tape to cover holes and fix vital parts of hats and clothing is not uncommon. Hiking boots or flip flops are the shoes of choice in the field. Of course, none of this is really acceptable in the office, and buying new clothes with our meager salaries wasn't really an option. Every day before getting dressed for the office I had to check the back and crotch areas of my jeans for holes. If my boxers weren't showing I would call it a success. Then there were my shirts. I would often go through two or three shirts before I came to one that did not have stains or holes in it. Finally, I needed to find a decent pair of shoes. Having never been big on dressing up even in college, I owned a pair of tennis shoes, a pair of boots, and one pair of old dress shoes. That was all. Obviously, I went with the tennis shoes. So after getting dressed in proper office attire I would head in to stare at my computer screen all day. This part of the job reminded me a lot of the movie "Office Space."

Dressing for the office was difficult, but there were still other adjustments to be made for city life. One was that I was used to urinating whenever I felt the need. I would simple walk out of view, take care of business, and then come back. Suddenly, finding a restroom every time I needed to go seemed like a ridiculous waste of water, especially since we were all trained to drink large amounts of water all day from working in the desert. I finally knew something was wrong when I decided to go in the corner of my friend's back yard rather than go inside the house to use the restroom. It was night time and we were grilling. After a few beers I needed to go, but to fight through the dogs, go inside, and chance having to wait in a line just seemed like a waste of time. So I slinked off over to the corner while everyone was talking, then came back. "Did you just piss over there!" someone said loudly. Confused, I nodded. Suddenly it was a huge deal. Again, it was something I did not really think about until after that night.

There were other small changes I had to make. For meals at camp and in the field we didn't carry napkins around. So yeah, the use of clothing was acceptable. So was eating off others plates, passing around a bottle for others to sample, and using the pan you cooked in as a plate. None of these went well at family dinners when I returned. My brother, who isn't the neatest of people called me out one day while I was eating. "You are not at camp anymore!" he yelled. I can't even remember what exactly I was doing to set him off, but I have no doubt I deserved it. We weren't slobs while we camped, but definitely had to adjust our manners after returning to regular society.

I also realized how much some people fear nature. While I am not a huge fan of bees, wasps, or spiders I learned to live in close proximity with them. Often, when in the restroom we would have to look for black widows or scorpions before using the facilities. On one such occasion I found a dead black widow with a bark scorpion in the web. Bees were always around our recycle bins in the desert, but we just got used to them. Lizards were a common site every day. When I visited my sister or parents I would often point out a spider or lizard from a distance and they would freak out. My roommate would shiver if I mentioned spiders, and my brother once missed a bus due to a bee hive near the bus stop. These things were just an everyday part of life in the desert.

***

After a month of data entry, my supervisors finally found a few side projects for me to work on. One of the projects was conducting deer browse surveys on the north rim of the Grand Canyon, which I was sure would be an incredible experience.

The Grand Canyon is one of the greatest natural wonders in the world, and the north rim is especially beautiful. It is also one of the coldest parts of Arizona in the winter and we were already in late fall. The surveys involved counting plants that had been browsed on by deer or other herbivores (essentially looking at leaves for bite marks). We were taking plant diversity data as well, looking at how many species occur at various parts of the area. It wasn't especially exciting work, but the scenery more than made up for it.

On one especially cold night, I happened to be at the farthest plot from the cabin when I got a flat tire. I was using a borrowed truck and thought I had done a good check for supplies. The truck contained a jack, but on closer inspection I discovered that the tire iron didn't match the lug nuts on the tire. I tried turning on the radio, and realized it didn't have any batteries. It was sunset, and the temperature was already below freezing. I wasn't really prepared to spend the night in sub-freezing temperatures, so I reluctantly started driving on the rim of the tire to look for help.

After about a mile or two I fortunately saw another one of our trucks. I hit the horn and flashed the lights. I was lucky, the other truck was only out to scout some areas for hunting, since they had finished their official work a few hours ago. We tried the tire iron from their truck, but it didn't fit either. There was nothing else we could do at this point but drive back to the cabin for the night. However, the cab of their truck was already full, so I had to enjoy a brisk, sub-freezing drive back to the cabin huddled in the bed of the truck. It was certainly an ignominious end to my first field season.

***

Those final Grand Canyon surveys marked the end of my first season as a field biologist. I definitely had some adventures: mountain lions, venomous snakes, kayaking through a spider forest, bird assaults, and two different truck problems. I went from surveying in 120-degree-plus heat to below-freezing temperatures, and met an amazing crew along the way. The hardest part of this job for me is saying goodbye when the season is over. Working and living with the same group of people brings you closer together. Some people seemed to deal with it better than others. Maybe it was tough for me because I just seemed to fit with these groups better than any others. Maybe it was because that first summer, with its newness and shocking change from what I was used to, was the most amazing and influential time of my life. I felt like every ten-day stint was a camping trip with a group of close friends. This also wouldn't be the first time I would get attached to the crew, knowing eventually the season would end and we would all go our separate ways. Some of us would meet again, but it would never be like it was. Over time, I would begin to adjust to all the travel, finding new places to live, and familiarizing myself with new plants and animals, but I've never gotten used to saying goodbye. No, it hurt every time and still does to this day.

2 From AZ to the O.C.

Near the end of my first field season with the Arizona Game and Fish Department, I landed a seasonal position with Audubon California conducting restoration work at Starr Ranch in Orange County, California. In preparation for my journey to California I had decided to give up my apartment—no sense in keeping a place if I did not know when I would be back. I did not know that this would be the last time I would have a place to myself for many years. One year after college most people are just starting to rent or buy their own places, and here I was giving mine up. I packed up everything I wanted to keep and took it to my parents' garage; the rest went to goodwill or the dumpster. I had half a dozen boxes of clothes and books in my vehicle that I had decided to take with me to California. When I pulled away from the apartment complex that day, my car then became my second home for the better part of the next decade.

It had been six months since I started my first field season, and I felt I had been through the wringer. Nothing could phase me—at least that's what I thought until I hit the California state line.

Suddenly, the nervousness was back. This was going to be the longest I had ever stayed outside Arizona. I had not traveled outside the state much—or anywhere really—and had no idea what to expect. I had never lived with anyone besides my best friend or my family. Now I was going to be sharing a five-bedroom cabin with the crew I was going to be working with. I spent most of the drive thinking over all the experiences I had had in just the first six months, and imagined the ones I would have with the rest of my life ahead of me. I was so optimistic then, and loved life on the road. I loved seeing new places and meeting new people, and thought those feeling would last forever.

***

The drive seemed to take an eternity, but I finally made it to Orange County. I pulled up to the address I was given—it was a hillside full of large mansion-like homes. A large golf course was within this community, and fancy cars, all sparkling clean, lined every home. As I looked at the squashed bugs on my windshield and the dirt covering the rest of the car a thought occurred to me for the first time in a while: "I should have washed my car." As I started to pull into this community I was stopped at a large gate and greeted by a security guard. He eyed my car, and after a long pause, finally asked me who I worked for. I replied Audubon California. He nodded like I had confirmed his suspicions, gave me a special sticker to get through the gate in the future, and then let me in. "Go directly to the last street on the right," he said, greatly emphasizing "directly." At this point I was thoroughly confused. Where was the preserve I was to work on? Had I unintentionally accepted a job as a gardener?

I proceeded to the last street on the right. The million dollar homes gave way to an overgrown, winding dirt road. I was probably one of the few people that would have been relieved to leave the large homes behind. A posted private property sign sat at the boundary of the preserve. This was more like it. I continued down the road to my future home.

***

Starr Ranch, my new home for the next few months, was a

property held by Audubon California. It was a former cattle ranch with a summer home built on the property. It was owned by and named after a wealthy Californian, and later acquired by Audubon California. My job was to help restore the property to the surrounding native—and endangered—coastal sage scrub habitat. It bordered a wealthy community on one side and national forest land on the other—an interesting set up. The restoration work involved mapping invasive plant species, using manual methods to remove them, and planting seeds of native plants. Manual removal was unheard of anywhere else at the time for a property this big. Most believed chemicals were a necessary part of habitat restoration, which is why Starr Ranch was so different.

When I pulled up to the Starr's former summer home, it definitely didn't seem like a place wealthy people would live. It was a small red cabin with a fireplace and large wood pile out front. It also had a clothes line in the front yard and a compost heap with a metal screen over it. It looked like something I might own someday, not something millionaires had once lived in. Still, it had a charm to it that couldn't be matched. It was also a step above most field housing I have had over the years.

Since I was the second to last of the crew to arrive I was given the choice of the two worst rooms of the house: the converted attic that had its own entrance or what seemed to be a large closet converted into a "bedroom." The closet was in the main house and near the fireplace and kitchen, but the attic had privacy—or so I thought. Unfortunately, I chose the attic.

The attic really wasn't horrible except for three things. The first was the floor boards; every move I made could be heard from the kitchen downstairs. This made me self-conscious about working out, getting up at night to use the restroom and—as I awkwardly found out later—activities with the opposite sex.

The second problem with the attic was my private bathroom. The roof of the house, like most, was slanted. This essentially meant I had an eight-foot-high ceiling near my bed, but a five-and-a-half-foot ceiling in the bathroom. I am six feet tall. I did not think much about this when I moved in, but after the first night I knew it was going to be a problem. Every guy probably could relate to what I am talking about. When you wake up in the middle of the night needing to pee, you are basically a zombie. You stumble forward, straight to the bathroom, bumping off obstacles as you go. I hit my head no less than six times the first week. Each time hurt just the same as the last. No matter how many times it happened, the next night I would hit it again. I never asked, but I am sure it amused the people below me, hearing a bump in the night followed by some soft swearing. I hated that bathroom. I often imagined whoever designed it was an evil genius who did it intentionally for their own amusement.

The last problem was probably the most embarrassing. First, let me explain that the stairs to my room were homemade by the handyman who greeted me the first day wearing a fake mullet. They were slightly uneven, narrow, and creaked eerily. I wasn't worried about walking up them but I also didn't want to test them with running or sudden movements.

At the top of the stairs was just enough room to open the door, and next to that door was a light that sat about face-level. On this light fixture that was face-level lived a colony of wasps, yellow paper wasps that got very angry whenever the door opened or closed. Seeing that I am not the biggest fan of wasps, but did enjoy being able to enter my own room at will, this was going to be a problem. I also thought it would be inappropriate to use chemical spray seeing how much emphasis and pride was put into being a non-chemical ranch. It seems silly now, but I was young and so eager to do a good job I did not want make a fuss about anything. So after several mad dashes down the dilapidated stairwell and nearly killing myself several times, I had found a routine, a truce with the wasps. I woke up before sunrise when it was cool out and the wasps were inactive, and exited my room. I would then wait until after sunset before returning to my room. I packed my after-work clothes and whatever else I thought I may need for the afternoon that morning. I was too embarrassed to tell the others why I did not go upstairs after work. I let them assume I was just lazy and avoided stairs when I could. This went on for a few weeks, but then it was the wasps that broke the treaty. One night I was strolling upstairs, got to the door, and when I opened the screen door to the room, there on the corner of the door, was a new nest. They were expanding. Not acceptable. That night I broke the rules and purchased wasp spray. I used it once and then hid the can for the better part of the season. I was guilt-ridden for several days. I felt like I was disposing of a murder weapon when I finally drove several miles in the city to find a place to get rid of the can.

Finally my life was no longer dictated by an insect species. All things considered, I really liked the housing and greatly valued my time spent at the ranch.

***

The crew I worked with here was very different from the crew on my first job—or maybe it was me that was different. In any case, they seemed to be around the same age group and experience level as me. I mean, they still had stories from other states and countries, which further solidified my resolve to keep traveling, but we seemed to be on equal ground now that I had been in the field and had my own stories. The crew consisted of a crew lead, four technicians (including myself), a few staff biologists, and two interns. While I liked everyone on the crew, I spent most of my time with the two female interns and another ASU alumni. The interns were an interesting duo. One was a 21-year-old girl that graduated from college two years before most people, and the second was a girl with a master's degree that wanted to gain some ground-level field experience. Both were new to the field and got along great. They memorized the scientific names of plants by pretending they were Harry Potter spells. I'll admit, I liked both of them from the start. Then there was the ASU grad. He was a birder, but not like the ones I worked with before. He lived to see new birds; they were his passion.

The best part of the crew was that most of us drove beat-up, older cars. Really, anything that cost less than $20,000 at the time would have looked beat-up in the surrounding neighborhood. I loved the looks we got driving in and out of the gate. "Hippies," I'm sure they thought. I guess I should have been offended to be looked down on, but I was loving life at the time and just thought it was funny. Some of the community really liked us, though, and constantly looked for ways to help. Volunteers were never hard to find in Orange County.

***

Doing this job for a while, you tend to forget how strange the situation is. Not thinking, one day I ordered a pizza for delivery. I mean, we did have an address and we got mail. Looking back, I felt

34

bad for the young girl delivering the pizza. First, getting stopped at the security gate. Then, driving past all the nice houses to an overgrown dirt road that is like something out of a horror movie. After that, meeting someone in front of a cabin with no lights on in the middle of an oak woodland at night. Not to mention I hadn't shaved for a while and was wearing field clothes that may have looked like something a homeless man would have thrown away. She sat in her car a long while before finally walking to the front door of the cabin. I kind of imagined her calling her parents to say any last words or something like that, but more than likely she was just trying to confirm the address. I have never seen someone so happy to leave before.

***

The job itself was simple: walking sections of the property looking for invasive plants and manually removing them with hoes or large, heavy brush cutters. Some areas were so heavily invaded that we walked for hours, or even days, with brush cutters cutting thistle and other invasive plants. This wasn't simple gardening—we walked up and down steep slopes and through brush carrying equipment that definitely threw off our balance. We were forced to wear helmets, goggles, and ear plugs during those days. I often thought of leaving the helmet in the car because it was so hot and bulky. That is until one day I found a large piece of wood that had been flung by my coworkers brush cutter stuck in my face mask. After that I was Mr. Safety. We also took data, and on occasion, dug up a small but very resilient invasive plant called *Plantago* using a tool that was basically a screwdriver. I am sure the tool had a fancy name, but I can no longer remember what that name was. Overall, the work was good and actually had helped restore several acres over the years.

***

Plants weren't my only encounter at Starr Ranch. I was actually in the area during the same time that a mountain lion had killed several people on a forest trail in Orange County. During that time I often found myself walking the quarter mile to the interns' bunkhouse after work. They would invite some of the residents from the main house (that was the cabin I stayed in) over for dinner or board games, which I was learning was popular among field

35

biologists.

One night while walking to the intern's place I heard a horrifying sound: a high-pitched scream mixed with a gargling sound. I remember thinking of it as a much louder and horrible version of an alley cat. A cat…my heart stopped. I was about halfway to the intern's place when I realized it was a cat. A very large cat in heat. A mountain lion. Once again I found myself unarmed with a large predator nearby. And this one was feisty from the sounds of it.

As I did at the Salt River six months earlier, I walked while making as much noise as I could. It was near pitch-black that night, and while I never did see the lion, I heard it several times during my walk. I was constantly eyeing the thick tree line next to the main road. There was a small stream that paralleled the main road, and that stream was surrounded by oaks and willows, making it almost impossible to see through during the day, and even less so at night. I imagined eye shine several times only to find it was water on leaves reflecting light from my head lamp. I did not want to quicken my pace in fear of tempting the lion, but I certainly didn't slow down. No, I wanted this experience over as soon as possible, so I maintained speed and kept a watchful eye out.

That was one of the longest walks of my life, but it ended without incident. We heard it the next few days after, as well, yawling in the distance. The next morning I asked our resident mammal researcher about the camera traps he had set up around the ranch. Sure enough, there was a lion around, and he had several videos and photos of it. He then informed me that the lion had be seen on a camera trap less than 100 feet from the main trail at the same time I usually embarked on my walks to the interns' place. I thought about it: a mountain lion was walking parallel to me in the tree line while I was on the road and I never even knew about it. Great. Once again, my fellow biologists failed to inform me of the presence of a lion until after I asked about it. Funny how that goes. From then on, I decided driving wasn't such a bad idea, even if it was only a half-mile round trip.

***

The mountain lion encounter did not discourage me from trying to find more ways to gain experience working with different wildlife.

I began to try to venture out and get as much experience as I could by volunteering. I started to volunteer to check the mist nets at a bird banding station nearby. A mist net, as it sounds, is a thin, very tightly woven net hung up to catch birds flying in the area. It is stationary and usually put in migratory areas. This one was used to catch birds in order to put small metal bands on them so biologists could follow their movements and recruitment habits. Whenever a banded bird is caught in the net the band number is recorded and then called into a national database. I was new to banding and mist netting, and the birds I worked with the previous season were already banded for the most part. It was during one of the banding sessions that my fellow ASU alumni invited me to go birding.

Birding is just what it sounds like: going out and looking for birds. In this instance, we were searching for endangered California condors. This was one of my first outings with a hardcore birder and I learned a valuable lesson that day about their excitement level. This guy was usually quiet and non-confrontational during work. I had never heard him yell until that day.

We were driving to Ventura from Orange County, which was a long drive through the heart of L.A. It had been about half an hour since we had stopped talking and started listening to the radio. We were on a narrow highway with large trucks coming from the opposite direction. I will admit I was speeding, since I wanted to see the birds and try to beat the traffic back home. As I was concentrating on the road, my passenger suddenly lurched forward, thrusted his hand straight at my face, and screamed, "Merlin!" The shock of the sudden outcry from him combined with what appeared to be him throwing a left jab at my face caused me to swerve off the road and nearly collide with a telephone pole. I hit the brakes, gained control of the vehicle, and slowed to a stop. My heart was beating like crazy. I looked over and instead of worry on his face he had binoculars glued to it. He was still looking at the bird—the fact that we were almost in a fatal car crash a few seconds ago didn't even phase him! I wanted to strangle him so bad, but I admired his passion too much to complain. I simply gave him a moment to see the bird—and me to calm down—before starting back on the road.

We did end up finding our birds. We saw a flock of large black birds circling over a field shortly after reaching the Ventura area. After looking for a moment I came to the conclusion that those birds were turkey vultures circling with some small blackbirds flying amongst them. After pulling out my binoculars, I was in awe. There were turkey vultures out there, but they were not the birds I thought. They were the "little" blackbirds flying around the Condors. The condors were huge, bigger than I had ever imagined. Suddenly, I could see why the earliest settlers could believe these things might fly off with their cattle or children. With over nine-foot wingspans, they dwarfed the turkey vultures, and until that point were one of the largest birds I had seen in the wild. We watched them effortlessly soar in circles for about an hour before turning back. Even with the near-death experience, I was very glad my birder friend had included me this day. This was just another day I thought how incredible some of God's creatures really are, and how important it is to protect such unique wildlife.

***

One thing the desert lacked that I could not get enough of in Orange County was the fall colors. The desert is a beautiful place, but it's a harsh beauty. A fragile bloom, jagged peaks, and red rocks contrasting with blue skies. When it comes to flowers the desert is usually drab with an occasional good spring bloom of annuals and several cacti. If you are lucky you might have a second bloom following the summer monsoon rains. Actually, some of the most amazing sights I've seen have come from a desert spring bloom, but out in Orange County the real beauty came from the fall and early winter colors. The oaks had just started to change colors when I arrived, and by the end of my first month I was seeing the most amazing views—reds, oranges, and greens mixed together lining all the canyons and streams. From the some of the higher peaks you could see a line of colors, above that was a view of the surrounding city, and from the highest peaks you could even see the ocean. I would often find myself on the taller peaks looking over the city to the ocean and looking for the Channel Islands, which were visible on clear days. I was easily distracted, always looking at the clouds, trees, or the ocean. Being from the desert, the fall colors and the ocean view was new to me and being able to stare at it every day is one of my favorite memories from Starr Ranch.

***

One sad day we had a visitor on the ranch. While performing maintenance on our equipment we all heard something moving out by the wood pile. After hearing it again I went to investigate. I was shocked to see a bobcat sitting in front of the wood pile, calm as could be. It appeared that it was intent on hunting a mouse. After grabbing my camera I took a closer look at it, and let out a sigh. This creature was not healthy. Its rib cage showed, its stomach was sunken in, and it moved awkwardly. It was most likely hunting mice because it could no longer handle anything bigger. Watching this poor creature made me ache with pity. We called a wildlife rescue group who came to retrieve the animal but they said it did not look good. I have seen a lot of death in my line of work, from necropsies of deer and other animals to killing invasive species, or cleaning of fish. All that gore never really affected me, but the memory of that poor creature still haunts me today. I saw firsthand that nature is not always kind. It can be unforgiving and cruel and is to be respected in all its forms.

***

Over the first two months at the ranch, I had been spending more and more time with the interns, one intern in particular. We had been getting closer, and one rum-filled night we crossed the friendship line and started something else. It all started one night at a Christmas party. Until now we had been hanging out together any chance we had and it really just took a little push to get us past the friend zone. Ok, that and maybe the rum. After that we were inseparable. We cooked together, took walks through the ranch together, and made trips to the city together. Things were good.

We had started staying at the interns' house rather than the main house after work. This was a slight disappointment to me since I had recently won my war against the wasps. We had decided this after realizing how loud the attic floorboards really were. One morning at breakfast in the main house, the crew lead made an awkward comment about how much "walking around" we had done the previous night. That was the last night we both stayed in that room.

After that awkward morning, I rarely went to my room, and

when I did it was just to pick up clothing and such. I was really enjoying staying at the interns' place—it was less crowded and they had a really nice hammock in the front yard. I could sit in the hammock and watch the deer graze near the avocado trees. It was very relaxing.

One day I went out behind the bunk house, which was what the interns' house was called, and started relieving myself. The bunk house was just a few feet from the tree line, but was a few hundred feet from their bathroom and showers so it made perfect sense. As I was relieving myself I looked down and noticed the invasive plant, *Plantago*. I had spent days on my hands and knees pulling this plant up by its roots in the grassland areas of the ranch. It was a horrible plant. I decided to try my own control method on the plant. From that day forth for the next four months, I pissed on that group of plants in back of the bunk house at least once a day. I thought this would eventually kill the plant, but I was wrong. I had underestimated the resilience of the plant. It did not wilt or die. Instead, it thrived on the piss. It got greener and greener. Everything else from that spot had died except the *Plantago*. The piss plant persisted.

My experiment did accomplish one thing: when the temperatures started rising it made the entire back of the bunk house begin to smell like urine. There was a drought going on and so the area had not gotten washed away like normal, and the dirt was releasing a horrible odor. No one but me knew where it was coming from, or why. The *Plantago* won that round. I broke down and brought some buckets of water from the creek, to wash the area and eliminate the smell. I now had a record of 1-1 in my battles with nature at Starr Ranch.

***

All good things come to an end. By the end of the season, I was convinced I was in love with the intern, and we had decided to try a long-distance relationship. By then, she had been hired by the National Park Service to go to the Virgin Islands for sea turtle nest patrols. She was going to be housed in a four-star resort on St. Croix. I had applied to that job as well, and while I did get asked to interview, I was not offered the position. Instead, I was headed back to Arizona and Roosevelt Lake to help a graduate student with her fawn mortality study. While I was sad to see my girlfriend leave, I was also very jealous. She was going to be working with sea turtles on an island resort, while I was going back to 100-degree desert heat. When the time finally came, we had a tearful goodbye at the airport, but I vowed to visit her in the islands. I swear it wasn't just to go to the Virgin Islands and play with sea turtles; I really was going to miss her. Truthfully, I was scared to see her go, but I knew I couldn't ask her to stay.

And so my California adventure was over. Time to head home. It had been just over a year since I had arrived at Roosevelt Lake for my first field season and here I was going back again. I was hoping to travel somewhere new, but how could I refuse a job working with deer fawns?

3 Back to the Beginning Again

A lot went through my mind on the drive back to Arizona. As the live oaks faded into Joshua trees and then to saguaros I thought about whether my relationship would last, and about the experiences I just had in California. Most of all, I thought about my return to Roosevelt Lake, where I was going to be tracking and collaring deer fawns. This was exactly the kind of work I had thought about when I pictured what a wildlife biologist actually does.

I was staying in an old cabin that was being used periodically by various agency biologists. The cabin was on the opposite side of the highway from the lake and was about half an hour from the nearest small town. It was owned by the state of Arizona, but I was actually working for a University out of Texas. The cabin itself was nothing special. It was old, probably built in 1970s or 80s. It was located down a rough, five-mile dirt road that lead into a canyon. In the wash at the base of the canyon sat the cabin. A small creek ran about a hundred feet away from the back door. The creek was filled with riparian vegetation and a few cottonwood trees littered the canyon floor. The remaining area was populated with mesquite trees, creosote bush, and various species of cacti. The cabin was a stark contrast to the otherwise beautiful canyon landscape.

Inside the cabin were two bedrooms, a kitchen, and a living room. The bedrooms each had four bunks in them and not much else. The living room had an old couch with torn cushions, a computer desk, and a small TV on a plastic stand. The kitchen was pretty standard; just a fridge, sink, and stove. All seemed to be at least 20 years old.

That was my home for the next three months. If it hadn't been for the excitement of tracking deer fawns I would have been missing my old home in the green hills of Orange County.

When I finally arrived down the long dirt road to my new home I was greeted by a very unusual site. A short blonde girl stepped out of the cabin and introduced herself as my new supervisor and the graduate student running the project. She was undoubtedly cute, but the thing that caught my eye was the shirt she was wearing. A very tight fitting shirt with the words "Drink him cute" on it. Not at all what I was expecting for a research biologist, but over the years I learned you never know what to expect out of people in this line of work.

After the introductions I was given a short tour of the cabin. I learned that even though it was the middle of June in the desert we only had enough fuel to run the generator a few hours a day. This meant the cabin had limited air conditioning. This was not mentioned in the interview, but I could handle it. After all, I survived camping here the previous summer.

***

The work in this area was proving to be very difficult. I started each day driving down the long dirt road before 3 AM, and was working six days a week. The first task of every day was radio telemetry, which involved using a radio receiver to find the deer equipped with radio collars. While it sounds easy this was a difficult task with many obstacles.

The first obstacle of telemetry was the terrain. The management area was between Roosevelt Lake and the Four Peaks mountain range. Between those areas were numerous large canyons, hills, and washes. There were several roads we would drive, and we had several stops at set points along those roads. At each stop we would take telemetry readings and compass bearings on the animals. The receiver would beep louder when the antennae was pointing in the direction of the deer and softer when it was not. The problem was the radio signal bounced off the canyon walls and hills. This would give false signals from wrong directions or mask the signal entirely. After acquiring three good bearings in different directions we would then draw the lines going the direction of the bearings on a laminated map using the GPS points of our stops. Where the three lines met was the location of the deer. This was called triangulation. Because we needed compass bearing from all different directions it required driving our trucks up steep mountains and narrow canyon roads. The tops of the mountains and canyons were preferred to eliminate most obstacles between the receiver and radio collar. To take an accurate reading we had to stop the truck, turn it off, and stand in the bed. Often on the narrow dirt roads there was barely enough room to stop and get out of the truck without risk of stepping over the edge. Telemetry is much easier on flat, even terrain.

The second obstacle was the time of day required to do telemetry. Telemetry had to be done at night during the summer. Prior to my arrival several of the deer were found to be pregnant during the initial collaring. Those that were pregnant were given a vaginal implanted transmitter (VIT) to help determine when they gave birth to their fawns. Those transmitters had temperature loggers built in so when the temperature dropped below the normal body temperature of the mule deer it would give off a different signal. When the fawns came out, so did the transmitter, and after sitting outside the body the transmitter would decrease in temperature. This is where night telemetry came in. After sunrise the air temperature would quickly rise above the normal body temperature of the deer and so the transmitter would give off the normal signal. Driving narrow canyon roads at night proved time-consuming and nerve-wracking. Several of the canyon roads had drop-offs on one side of over 50 feet, and facing them at night did not make it any easier.

The last challenge of telemetry was the annoying habit of deer randomly moving far beyond their normal range. The deer mostly stayed in the same area, but once in a while they would move far beyond what was expected. Usually, when triangulating deer positions you have a few set spots to take your telemetry readings, so when the deer move on a tangent you can no longer get a good reading from your set spots. Then, you have to venture to new areas and essentially guess which direction the deer moved. I had mornings where I had to stop at ten different spots to get one good reading on a deer, and other mornings where I could not get a signal on the deer at all. The good thing is, under most circumstances, the signal of the missing deer eventually pops up.

Once the telemetry was finished we evaluated the data to determine if any of the deer may have dropped their fawns. If the deer were in the exact same spot for more than a day or two it usually meant they had a fawn nearby. If this was the case, we would drive to the last known area and check out the deer with a spotting scope. If the deer was located and did not look visibly pregnant, we would walk in on it to locate the fawn. We would also search the area where the deer was staying for evidence of birthing. Usually there was a wet spot and ants in the area if the deer had given birth. Walking in on the deer meant climbing up and down harsh desert landscaping, and there was rarely a clear path to the deer. Going up steep canyons and hills, through cactus and thorn scrub was pretty typical most days. It was exhausting work, but it always paid off when we found a newborn fawn.

***

I found my first fawn in early July, which was somewhat early for the mule deer in this part of the Sonoran Desert. We had gotten the signal from the VIT earlier in the morning and had set out as soon as the telemetry work was done. The signal came from high in the hills to the south of the lake. It took about an hour of hiking up and down steep hills and washes to get to the fawn. I was exhausted. My legs felt like Jell-O and I was already thinking about studying an animal that inhabited flat, cool areas next season. The temperature was well over 100 degrees and we were walking through a forest of cat-claw acacia.

We found the transmitter and birthing spot earlier in the hike, so we knew the deer was in the area. Though not very agile at first, mule deer are able to walk minutes after being born, so it was possible that the deer had left the area. Possible, but not likely, since the mother usually hides the fawn in tall grass or shrubs after birth for camouflage. We kept searching, and finally, I caught a glimpse of fur. The fawn was laying in some tall dry grass near a small shrub. It was still slightly wet and was covered by the traditional white spots. It was pretty much all legs. The body was half the size of its legs, and I couldn't help but think of Bambi. It was the cutest thing I had ever seen in the wild. I nearly shouted, but caught myself, knowing even now the fawn could run if alerted to our presence. I gave the hand signal to the others and got the equipment ready. It was time for the capture!

When dealing with some newborn wildlife, a biologist must be aware of the potential to accidentally imprint the animal. Imprinting is when the new animal forms a bond with the first creature it makes contact with after birth. This is usually the mother, but it can sometimes happen to a biologist when trying to process the study animal. Weighing, measuring, and putting on the radio collar can take a few minutes even when working quickly. Because of this, the animal's head is covered during the processing. That way, it can't tell who or what is interacting with it.

I stood poised over the animal clutching a pillow case, which I later learned were valuable with many different animal captures. I waited for the crew lead's signal. There it was! We all pounced on the creature. My adrenaline was flowing—I had not gotten to capture a live deer before. I dove for the head and threw the pillow case over the fawn. Even on our first fawn we had practiced enough and all moved with precise, calm, quick actions. It was over in seconds. The fawn was weighed, measured, and collared. Since it was the first fawn capture of the season, we all took a very quick picture with it. When we finished, we released the fawn unharmed, and retreated to watch its behavior for a few minutes. Upon observing that it was okay, we left the area. We had a successful capture, hopefully with many more to come. This was what I had imagined wildlife biology to be.

***

Snake encounters have always been a big part of my work outdoors. Most of the time it's been as simple seeing a snake while hiking or having one pass by while on a break (or hanging out near my kayak). My second season at Roosevelt Lake was no exception.

During that summer, I had multiple snake encounters, but three in particular have really stuck with me through the years. The first one occurred after a long day of telemetry and hiking. We had walked in on two deer that day, and the crew lead and I were exhausted and frustrated, since neither deer had actually given birth. It had been several days since we had collared a new fawn and we were getting impatient. It was late morning when we hit the long dirt road, and I was starting to doze off. We hit a large bump that jolted me awake and I looked ahead. At the same moment I saw a flash of brown and red drop from the sky in front of us. There was a flurry of motion and then the object took to the sky again. It was a red-tailed hawk. Seeing the hawk at that distance was impressive, but then I saw the prey dangling from its talons. It was a three-foot-long western diamondback rattlesnake. The hawk flew to a nearby mesquite tree, laid the snake on one of the limbs, and started to feast. It was an amazing site. We rolled to a stop and started to get our cameras out when the hawk took notice. I felt truly awful when the hawk took flight and left most of its prey uneaten on the tree limb. I took solace in knowing that it would more than likely return to finish its meal. It was the first—and so far—only time I've seen a hawk prey upon a rattlesnake in front of me.

The second snake encounter reminded me that not all biologists feel the same way about snakes. One morning, I was greeted with a visit from the cabin's caretaker, a wildlife manager from the state. It was good to have some company, so I offered to assist him with maintaining the property. While working I saw a large hole under an old cottonwood tree. Being the biologist that I was, I took a light and shined it into the hole. To my surprise, in the hole sat a large Mojave rattlesnake. Mojave rattlesnakes look a lot like western diamondbacks, but have a slightly different body coloration, and contain more white on the banded tail. Mojave rattlesnakes also have some of the most potent venom of all the rattlesnakes, containing both hemotoxins (which affect the blood) and neurotoxins (which affect the nervous system). While I stared at the creature in wonder (I had seen only a few of that species of rattlesnake at this point), the manager had walked up behind me and promptly cut the head off the snake with his tree loppers. I was enraged. This was a biologist. His duty, in my opinion, was to protect native wildlife. He had no intention of eating the snake and it was not in the city limits. There was no reason for his actions. He began to explain the dangers of rattlesnakes, but having many close encounters with them myself and never having felt in danger, I could not understand his actions. I was young at the time, and if I were there today I would have taken the challenge of debating his justifications. However, at that time I knew I just needed to leave the area and cool down. I never saw him again. I really don't blame him much anymore, since I have now come to realize that people are just raised to think that way. Still, it was disappointing to see that attitude from a biologist. Most biologists believe rattlesnakes are vital to a healthy ecosystem, and are to be respected, not feared.

My last memorable encounter came one cool morning after the monsoon rains had come. I had just finished breakfast, and had sat down on the front porch to tie my shoes. We had two chairs out there and I chose the one closest to the door. It was still dark, so before sitting I checked the top of the chair. I did not see anything so I sat, tied my shoes, and got up to leave for the day. After walking to the truck, I could not remember if I had locked the cabin door. I turned to head back when my headlamp caught eye shine from the porch. There, under the chair I was just sitting on, was a small Mojave rattlesnake. My hands had to have been only inches from its face when I was tying my shoes, and yet, I was not bitten. Perhaps the snake was too cold to strike, or I had just been really lucky. Either way, it was something I won't ever forget, and it reminded me to be vigilant even while performing normal, mundane tasks in the field.

∗∗

Trusting who you work with is essential in field biology. I had not really thought about that much until the day I almost died.

During my first year of field work, the department had required me to take an extensive off-highway training course. The course covered everything from rock crawling to driving in sandy conditions, and even how to get unstuck from any situation. This course, combined with the experience I had gained with my first two jobs made me very comfortable driving in almost any situation. It did not, however, help me feel the same way being a passenger.

One day, after walking in on a new fawn, I was riding back to camp with the crew lead. It had been a long, hot day. Her boyfriend had decided to accompany us in the field that day, and I was in the back seat. We were on a narrow mountain road near the southern extent of the site, nearly into the Four Peaks area. To our left was a solid rock wall and to the right was a steep 50-foot drop-off. While making a tight turn around a rocky outcrop next to the road we suddenly lurched forward. The whole truck tilted to the right. I heard a loud clunk. My heart raced. Things seemed to move in slow motion. I looked forward and saw our truck was slightly off-center of the road. This was not good. There was no room for error. She had not taken the turn tight enough. The truck lurched forward slightly more. Then another clunk. This time I felt it, the rocks had caught on the transfer case. I breathed a slight sigh of relief—at least we were safe for the moment. I was on the left side of the vehicle so I did not want to exit before the person on the passenger side. Slowly he climbed in the driver seat as the driver exited the vehicle. Then I exited and he did as well. We were safe. The crew lead began to speak: "I don't know what happened..." she began. I cut her short, shouting "YOU DROVE OFF THE CLIFF!" I stopped there, figuring that blaming her wouldn't help anyone. We began to evaluate the situation.

The truck's right tire was over the edge, and the truck had slid slightly that direction until the transfer case had gotten hung up on some rocks. It appeared the truck was stuck solid and not going over the mountain, but that also meant we were not getting it unstuck either. Our cell phones had no real service, and could only send out text messages. After a short discussion, we started walking down the mountain. It was only a couple miles to the highway and all downhill.

After reaching the highway, we hitchhiked to the nearest gas station where we waited for a tow truck. We sat mostly in silence. The tow truck arrived and took us back up the mountain. When we arrived, the driver started shaking his head and said, "No way we getting this out with just one truck." Soon, a sheriff's department truck arrived with a heavy-duty winch. It took nearly an hour to get the truck back on the road. We all felt very lucky that night.

Since that day, I have always been nervous about field partners. In this line of work you find yourself working around dangerous creatures, roads, and tools, often in remote areas. A single careless mistake by a crewmember could mean dire consequences for the rest of the crew. I now find myself very cautious of new people until they prove themselves.

***

A few days after the truck incident we had our first fawn mortality. It was a sad day when I got the signal indicating death. It was sad, but also expected—this was a fawn mortality study, after all. I am usually pretty good handling death in the wild. I see it has part of a cycle. *The Lion King* taught me that. But I was not prepared at all for what I saw that morning.

The radio collars on the deer gave off a unique signal when death occurred. Each collar has a motion sensor built in. When no motion is detected for 24 hours, the animal is more than likely dead and the transmitter emits a different signal. It is important to find the carcass as soon as possible to avoid scavengers moving the carcass and causing the collar to give off a live signal again.

We were preparing for the hike in when the crew lead went back to the truck to get equipment. When she returned, this petite blond girl had a .44 magnum hand gun strapped on her hip. The gun was half the size of her thigh. When I asked about the gun she informed me that we were walking in on a possible mountain lion kill and had to be prepared. I this was fine until I thought about it a little later. Often, we separated when hiking. What if I get attacked when she isn't around? State policy dictated that since I was a tech I was not allowed to carry a gun. I just hoped the mountain lion's policy dictated that they don't attack techs, only supervisors. When the season got busier we spread out more on fawn and kill searches. I was unarmed on those searches, at least to their knowledge. I actually started carrying my own .357 magnum when I worked alone. However, on this initial fawn mortality I was unarmed.

When we drew near the fawn, the habitat had changed from desert scrub to a large swath of hills covered in cholla cactus. This was teddy bear cholla—or jumping cholla, as some call it—and in my opinion, the worst kind of cactus. The cactus is segmented, with each segment containing hundreds of barbed spines an inch and a half long. When an animal even slightly brushes by the cactus the barbed spines catch the animal and the entire segment releases from the cactus. The weight of the segment then causes even more spine punctures. Our signal was coming from the middle of the cholla-covered hills.

After carefully picking our way through the cactus patch, we eventually came to the fawn. When we found it we all gasped. This was not a coyote or lion kill. The fawn was covered from head to hoof in cactus spines. There was a segment attached to the deer's face with spines puncturing the deer's eyeball. It was hard to even move the fawn with the amount of cactus covering it. After a difficult necropsy (an animal autopsy) we found no other marks or causes of death. It was the cactus that killed the fawn. A horrible way to go. The theory we came up with was the fawn was bedded down near the area and something spooked it. It jumped and ran the opposite direction of whatever spooked it, and straight into the cactus area. Once in the area the deer panicked when the spines stuck in and it thrashed around impaling itself further. Whatever happened, I never looked at teddy bear cholla the same way. I was learning how dangerous the desert can be—even the native animals can't afford a moment of panic.

***

It was late in the summer and the desert was starting to get to me. I had been on a strange schedule of working early in the morning, followed by trying to sleep during the hottest parts of the day. The AC to the cabin was still only being run a few hours a day, mostly right after we finished work in the morning so we could enter our data into the computer in relative comfort. I had also found out after the monsoon rains that our cabin was infested with bark scorpions, which are the smallest and most venomous scorpions in the United States. They are also the best climbers. I had found scorpions in my bed, the toilet, the sink and next to my alarm clock after I had just hit the snooze button. Often, they were the last thing I saw on the ceiling before shutting my eyes for a few hours of sleep—or attempts at sleep, anyway. I was hot and dehydrated all the time. I was also lonely.

It was August and I finally decided to do it: I was going to fly to the Virgin Islands to visit my girlfriend. The first obstacle was finding the money. I had already built a nice credit card debt buying field equipment and traveling. Making $8 an hour was definitely not going to buy me a ticket, so I began to sell just about everything of value I owned: video games, movies, and anything else I could think of. I rarely used anything other than my field gear and my computer so I really wasn't going to miss much. Looking back, visiting the Virgin Islands and the adventures I had there were well worth it.

A week after I decided I needed out of the desert, I had my plane ticket. The scope of what I was doing didn't really hit me until I saw the ocean under the plane. I had just decided to leave the desert and fly thousands of miles to the Caribbean on a dehydrated whim. I didn't care, but it was definitely the most impulsive thing I had done. I thought about the seeing sea turtles for the first time, swimming in the ocean, and of course seeing my girlfriend.

One of the most memorable things of the trip was the billboard I saw while landing. It said "Home of Tim Duncan." I was a huge Phoenix Suns fan and I hated Time Duncan. Kind of a random memory, but it definitely stuck.

After my girlfriend picked me up, we went straight to her field housing. At this point in my career I had lived in a tent, a dilapidated attic, and a scorpion-infested cabin. I then looked at her housing: a four-star resort with a private beach, king size bed, and all the AC you could want. I was quickly contemplating how much I liked sea turtles.

On my second night in the islands, I decided to accompany the crew on the night beach patrol. I was again blown away by the difference in their work. We took a patrol boat to an uninhabited island, which was also a national park. The park was closed to the public after dark, which was when we did our sea turtle patrols. We then walked the three miles of beach looking for nesting turtles. The island's beach was quickly eroding, so when a turtle nested too low on the beach the crew relocated the nest to a safer spot. This was more often the case than not. The process seemed simple in theory, but I soon learned firsthand that sea turtles lay huge amount of eggs, which meant relocating the nest wasn't the easiest thing in the world.

On the following night of patrols, I was walking the beach like before. The beach was rather narrow with thick tropical vegetation only a few meters off the shoreline. It had been a busy day from what I could tell. We still had not seen our own turtle. Then about half way in the night I saw it: a green turtle the size of a kitchen table working its way on the beach. I couldn't believe I was seeing anything so large and amazing so close in the wild. It was dark, so I could not see the details of the creature very well. Lights disorient sea turtles, so cameras and flashlights were out of the question. We followed it onto the shore until it picked a spot only a few feet from the vegetation line and started to dig. My girlfriend shook her head—this was not a good spot. A second turtle had been spotted a little ways away and required her attention, so I was given the task of collecting the eggs for relocation.

I was finding that every field job, no matter how amazing it sounds, has certain parts that are difficult. I was sitting in back of a 100-plus pound turtle collecting eggs. This may sound great, but I was literally catching eggs has they came out of the cloaca (basically an all-purpose hole for defecation and reproduction found in all reptiles, amphibians, and birds). They were slimy and had a distinct smell to them. Still, it was something few people ever get to see, and even less get a chance to help out with. The eggs had begun to come out faster than I could catch them. They were building up at the bottom of the hole the turtle had dug. I was in awe at how many there were. There had to be nearly fifty. The turtle stopped. I leaned deep in the hole to try and get the last few eggs. Then...poof! I was hit in the face with sand. I was stunned. Then again, sand in my face. The turtle was burying the nest. I tried to work faster but I was mostly blinded from the sand in my eyes. I could barely see but I am pretty sure the turtle gave a smirk before pelting me again. It is very surprising how much sand those turtles can move. I was desperately digging in the hole, trying to get the last egg out. I was completely blind now and just feeling for it. Finally I felt the leathery egg and gently placed it in the bag. I retreated and let the turtle finish its work. I washed my eyes out and watched as the turtle made its way back to the ocean.

Seeing the monster sea turtles on land wasn't the only amazing site in the Virgin Islands. I would sit for hours watching the thunderstorms over the ocean. Buck Island had no electricity and during the night was closed to the public. Those two things combined with the vast ocean surrounding it made the beach the best stargazing spot I had ever been too. I sat and watched shooting stars for hours during my time there. The desert sky is certainly amazing, but I think I found its equal that trip.

During one of my last days on the islands, I volunteered to go on a patrol of the resort beaches. This was part of the agreement for free housing between the resorts and national park service. Sea turtle patrols would be done once a week. As I was walking, I noticed strange tracks in the sand. I called up the crew to have them take a look. Then I noticed something in the sand: a small, grey object moving, mostly covered in sand. As I looked closer I realized it was a hatchling turtle. This was a nest emergence. Those were turtle tracks. After the crew arrived, we sifted through the sand and found several more hatchling turtles. This was the leftover of a nest emergence. Sometimes, not all of the little guys make it out at once. These were the endangered leatherback sea turtles—a very uncommon find—so we spent the rest of the evening helping little baby sea turtles make their way out of the sand to the ocean. It was a perfect end to my vacation.

***

My field season at Roosevelt Lake ended not long after I returned from the Virgin Islands. I had a long talk with my girlfriend and we had decided to both go for a large reptile and amphibian monitoring project in the Ozarks of Missouri. We both were quickly developing a love of reptiles and amphibians, and since the job involved studying them, it seemed like a perfect fit. It wasn't long after we had applied that we both got job offers. We were going to be working together again, but both of us would be totally out of our elements in the large deciduous forests of southern Missouri.

Packing up and leaving the cabin did not take long. I had a few months before my job started in Missouri and I had only one place to stay until then…I was going to live with my parents.

4 The Times Between

It was after my second season at Roosevelt Lake that I began to realize the true nature of this work. Really, it is not just a career, but a way of life. My job had ended at the lake and my next position did not start for six months. This left a lot of time in between.

When pursuing a life as a wildlife biologist you must understand that thousands of people graduate each year from schools all around the country, and only a few of them land a full-time, permanent position. There are only a very few permanent positions available, most of which are with government agencies. Once in a permanent position, people rarely leave it. So, there comes a time when even the most experienced biologist cannot find work in their field. When these times come you take whatever job comes your way. I have been in these circumstances and have been forced to make money anyway I could.

In the middle of the 2000s, a great recession hit the United States and forced me to reconsider my career. I was between field jobs and was looking for work. I found myself applying to department stores, gas stations, and restaurants with no luck. My resume had very few skills that meant much to the service industry. Telling people you can handle venomous snakes, use a tranquilizer gun, and set up a drift fence in an interview for a gas station attendant just gets you funny looks. It also was the first time I found my degree hurt my chances of a job. Most service industry places knew that as soon as I found a better position I would quit, so they refused to hire me. Money was scarce and my debt began to climb. If it wasn't for my parents allowing me to stay in their home for free it would have been a scary situation.

Even with the generosity of my parents I still needed money. I had to find some creative ways to make extra cash. The first thing I thought of was selling some of my wildlife photos. After several attempts, I quickly learned people are not willing to pay much for wildlife photos and there were better photographers out there than myself. After that I began to sell anything I did not need on eBay— books, old field gear, some of my parents' old junk they no longer cared about. This did not amount to much, but every penny counted. I was quickly learning that selling objects was not going to cut it.

Selling my belongings wasn't the only way to make money while unemployed. I had also resorted to selling my bodily fluids. Well, not all of them. I was selling plasma. I was a blood donor until this point, but I knew I could not do both. Selling plasma is not fun. You sit in a room, usually with a bad movie playing in the background, with a needle in your arm. Your blood is taken out, the plasma is removed and the red blood cells are pumped back in your arm. It usually took me about 90 minutes to complete the donation. 90 minutes with a needle in my arm, twice a week. The money wasn't great, but it at least paid for gas and food for a few days.

***

There were several times in my career that I was forced to work jobs that were outside my area of study. One of these was working as a delivery driver for my dad's small business. His business was shipping freight from the major shippers to rural parts of Arizona that not many people knew how to navigate in. I delivered to several of the reservation areas and small mining towns in eastern Arizona. This was before GPS navigation for cars had become popular. The only way to navigate to these outposts was through maps and directions from the locals.

My first few weeks I spent loading and unloading freight in the warehouse, which didn't have heat or AC. Even when taking a job in the city I still could not escape the elements. I quickly learned I was not suited for this line of work. I meticulously sorted and organized my freight and tried to help others grab their freight as the packages rolled down the conveyor belt. One day I looked around the warehouse. People would drop freight marked fragile straight on the ground from the belt. Packages were thrown around, stepped on, and even kicked. After weeks of observing the lack of care of the freight, one incident still took me by surprise. As I was loading my truck getting ready to leave for the day I heard a commotion. One of the other subcontractors had backed into someone's already sorted pile of freight. Heated words were being exchanged and then the truck just left. That wouldn't have been any different than a normal day until the contractor whose sorted pile had been knocked over began to chase the truck out of the ware house screaming and throwing packages at the truck along the way. It looked like something out of a cartoon. I could not believe what I was seeing. I had to take a minute to make sure it had really happened. Someone was throwing customer's packages at a work truck speeding out of the warehouse. I made sure to put extra padding in anything I shipped from then on.

While working for my father I heard many stories from the other drivers. Ranging from cute girls answering the door to half-naked women inviting the drivers in. I was very hopeful when I started as a driver. That hope quickly vanished. Not only was there no half-naked women greeting me at the door, on more than one occasion it was a three hundred pound man with no shirt on answering. I was glad to be working, but relieved when I was finally able to quit.

***

Later in my life I found myself debating about going back to school and possibly going into another line of work. At this point, I had been working several years as a wildlife biologist and I had no health insurance or savings account. Seeing that living in rural areas and traveling often increases the chances of all sorts of accidents, I was beginning to worry about my future. I also was having a hard time finding my next field job. So, I began to apply to jobs in the city.

After some help from a friend I was hired as a medical imaging assistant. I was assisting the technician that preformed CT scans. My job essentially was moving patients from the Emergency Room to the CT room. Once there I would help move the patient to the exam table. I quickly realized I worked much better with animals.

I worked nights in the ER, so I found myself dealing with many interesting people. Coincidentally, right about closing time for the bars was when we got the busiest. We also were near a retirement community. During my time working there I was spit on, swung at, nearly shit on, and called every name you can think of, usually by drunk or elderly people. Drunk elderly people were the worst. I could handle animals biting and shitting on me, but dealing with sick humans was too much. I was also starting to greatly miss the outdoors. So, I gave up going back to school, rode out the job until the first available wildlife position became available, then packed up my tent and hit the road again.

5 Long Way from Home

After a few short and interesting months living with my parents and working with my father, the time had come for me to move on. I was off to Missouri to survey and trap reptiles and amphibians in the Ozarks. This job would be taking me the farthest from home since starting this career. It would also be my first time handling venomous reptiles and working with amphibians. I was excited.

After two and a half days of driving, I finally found myself on a wildlife preserve in the heart of the Ozarks. I had arrived with my girlfriend and I was relatively surprised that she retained such a title after sharing a car together for roughly 32 hours. Nevertheless, we were here and everything was new, from the deciduous forest to the traditional four-season climate. The most exciting experience for me was working with new species of herpetofauna (a collective group of reptiles and amphibians). So, my adventure in the Midwest began.

***

In the months before beginning my adventure in Missouri, all I would hear from people was how cold it gets in the winter. I heard horror stories of below-freezing days and how my desert-adapted body would not survive the winter. I listened to their advice. I brought thermal underwear, sweaters, jackets, and a sub-zero-degree face mask. I also brought snow gloves and zero-degree boots. The day of my arrival in Missouri it was 65 degrees and sunny. I was not impressed. It was colder in Phoenix, Arizona, than Winona, Missouri.

After spending the week mocking the "cold" weather, karma showed up. The next week it dropped to highs in the 30s, and the week after that began the worst ice storm in 50 years. Trees were being toppled from the weight of the ice, something I didn't know happened. Our homemade basketball court was coated in over an inch of ice. I guess I deserved it.

After the storms stopped the ice remained. While working in a remote wildlife preserve you use your vehicle a lot less often than in the city. There aren't many places to go and the nearest town is over an hour away, so you stock up on supplies. One evening, after the ice storms I went out to the car to grab something out of the back seat. What I was after I no longer remember. What I do remember was standing in front of the car confused as to why my key wouldn't fit. Then with a little light I saw the reason: there was at least an inch and a half of ice coating the entire car. I had never seen this before. I had no idea how to deal with it. I went back inside and began to complain to my roommate, a native Missourian. "What the hell? Do you just not use your cars 'til spring?" He laughed at that. Soon after, I rigged a portable heater to a chair outside and pointed it at the car door. This brought more laughs, but it worked. After an hour, I was able to get inside. Later I was shown how to crack the ice with the ice scrapper. This didn't happen in the Sonoran Desert.

Later, during the same ice storms we lost power. This was much more serious than not getting into my car. We had no heat, no water and all the roads out were steep and coated with ice. After much debate we brought out snow chains and made a run to the field housing in the next town over for a few days. Power had been lost to cities all over Missouri. In the desert, a power outage means you may be hot, but it never seemed life-threatening before. I was learning every rural area had its own set of dangers.

The ice storms weren't all bad. They led to an invention of a new sport, probably one of the least safe sports you could think of, and one that no kid should ever play. We called it "Ice Basketball." The game is exactly what the name implies; we played basketball on ice. Dribbling was kind of optional, no fouls were called, and really, most of the time you were just trying to stay on your feet. No skates were allowed, only shoes. I think every one of us came in with a few new bruises the day we played, but after being cooped up in the house for so long during the storms we had to do something. It turned out to be a lot of fun. The storms had occurred less than a month after my arrival, and I began to wonder what else Missouri had in store for me.

***

The project I had drove out here for was a long-term ecological monitoring project. It was the Missouri Ozark Forest Ecosystem Project (MOFEP). This project was looking at the effects of even age forest management (clear cutting for logging), uneven age management (cutting some older trees and leaving others), and a control site (no logging at all). In addition to the herp crew I was on, there was also a bird crew and a vegetation crew.

The first few months of the job—after training—consisted of installing our herpetofauna traps. These were five gallon buckets buried to the lip with three-foot-tall sheets of tin running three directions from the bucket. Funnel traps were placed at the ends of the walls of tin. The idea was that a lizard, snake, or amphibian traveling through the forest hits the wall of tin. The metal is too slick for the animal to climb over, so it either follows the tin to the buried bucket (pitfall trap) or to one of the funnel traps. The tin was arranged to go out at 120-degree intervals from the center of the bucket.

While it sounds simple enough to install 84 of these traps, we quickly realized there was nothing simple about it. To install the tin you need to dig three trenches, each approximately eight inches deep, which wouldn't be a problem if we weren't in a forest. Time after time we hit huge roots that we would have to cut through. Other times we would take a big swing with a pick and be jarred to the bone after hitting solid rock. This of course was after a few weeks of digging in frozen ground. By the end of the first few months I had developed a mighty hump on the right side of my back. Whether muscle from swinging the pick right-handed, or scar tissue from the impacts of hitting rock and root I have no idea, but it stayed with me for a few months.

Once the traps were in place the job got much more interesting. We were doing marked recapture for this study. We marked the captures by toe clipping, which basically involved clipping the ends of the toes from the species caught. Before anyone lectures on animal rights, know that most amphibian and reptile species are capable of growing their limbs back and have far fewer pain sensors than most mammals. The toes were clipped in a unique order to help with identification if the animal was recaptured. Afterwards, the animal was released. This marking and recapturing process helped get accurate population estimates for the animals we were studying.

***

Coming into this project I had never really worked with reptiles and amphibians before, but more importantly, I had never worked with "herpers" before. I guess a decent analogy in my mind is that herpers—people who look for all manner of reptiles and amphibians in their spare time—are the rock stars of the biological community. The birders I worked with were usually early to bed, mild-mannered characters. Birders also seem to have their own unique sense of humor, which I call "bird humor." The mammal people are usually people who love the cute and fuzzies. They got into it for what we call the charismatic megafauna (big cats, small mammals, bears, wolves, etc.). That, or they are hunters and have a broad appreciation for the outdoors.

Most herpers I have met are always ready to have a beer at the end of the day, stay up all hours of the night, and are ready to do it again the following day. I remember some of the crew playing beer pong for more than half the night, and if the weather was ideal they would be up at sunrise ready to look for the first basking reptiles.

Missouri is an ideal place for herpers. There are plenty of snakes and salamanders that cross the roads and there are plenty of back roads on which to find them. It also didn't hurt that Missouri did not have an open container law, which made road cruising for snakes even more fun. Road cruising is just what it sounds like: you drive down roads which have habitat on both sides and look for animals (mostly herps) either crossing the road or just hanging out. It is also used to survey for very mobile animals, as well, such as many of the large mammals of Africa.

After a few months of working I was becoming more and more of a herp nerd. I found myself looking up facts, reading old text books, and going out road cruising several times a week. It finally hit me one morning how far I had gone. The night before, all the girls on our crew of 17 had gone away for the weekend, and the guys decided to have a drinking night. The night started out as people might imagine a night of drinking with six mostly single guys in their early to mid-twenties. We talked about the girls on the crew, past stories of traveling or college, but then the night took a turn. Suddenly we were talking about frogs and who has seen which species. More and more shots of alcohol were taken and more talking was done. That's the last I remember of the night. I woke up that morning and found the guys in the kitchen crowded around one of their cameras. I went to see what the commotion was over. There, on the screen, was one of my roommates standing in what we had deemed the poop pond, holding a spring peeper (a species of frog). The poop pond was really just a reclamation pond outside the field housing. We called it the poop pond because it had an awful smell. It really wasn't too bad, but it made for good jokes. After I saw the picture I began to laugh. "Really!? You really went out there!? That's kind of gross." I said. After my statement I got some strange looks. I felt a pit in my stomach. Then, they scrolled through the pictures, stopping on a specific one. Sure enough, there I was, ankle deep in the poop pond holding a frog with a goofy, drunken look on my face. When did this happen? I wondered. It had finally happened; I was one of them. Truth be told, I was glad I went out there, as it looked like I was having a great time. Since then, I have been thoroughly fascinated with reptiles and amphibians.

***

Our housing was basically six gutted and remodeled trailers with halls connecting them. The first trailer housed the bathrooms. They were dorm-style, with shower stalls, several toilets, and several sinks. Then there were the living trailers, which were standard bunk-style rooms, four bunks to a room. I was rooming with my girlfriend. The next room over was my good friend and roommate KJ. Further down was the full-time caretaker and ecologist, HM. They were good roommates and we all got along well. Throughout the year we had Americorps kids come in to do invasive species control, and during the summer we had a bird crew, but mostly it was just us three. The rest of the herp crew stayed in the other field housing about 55 minutes away. It was set up the same, except they were five minutes from town, while we were an hour away. Their housing was also much more crowded, one reason I was thankful to be where I was.

Outside the housing was the reclamation pond. The housing was set in a cleared field, and a few hundred feet away was the forest. Huge stands of oaks and other deciduous trees surrounded our housing. It was strange being surrounded by trees. It was also strange to arrive and see the forest go from completely bare in winter to almost impassable in the summer, and then fade to fall colors. Being from the desert, I was used to being the tallest thing around. You could always get your bearing and see what was coming. That all changed out here. My compass became the main source of navigation. GPS usually couldn't pick up satellites, and there were few hiking trails. It became a whole new way to navigate.

A little ways down from the house was a small creek and clean pond. We could always hear the spring peepers calling from here. On occasion we would hear some of the tree frogs or other species calling. Usually, that meant a trip out with the head lamps to find what was calling.

Beyond the stream was the field station. This was where the permanent staff worked during the day. They all had homes they went to after work, which sounded nice, since that was something I hadn't had since college.

***

So many things were different in Missouri; the habitat was different, the crew was different, and the animals were definitely different. One of the most common snakes in that area of Missouri was the copperhead. This is a venomous pit viper, but unlike rattlesnakes, this one had no rattle.

This snake, along with several other venomous snakes in Missouri, blended so seamlessly with the leaf litter on the ground that on more than one occasion I found myself sitting or standing next to one without ever noticing. One of the more memorable times this happened was early in the season coming back from checking my pitfall traps.

I was walking through the dense forest, and could hear the crunches of dried leaves with every step. I was going cross country, now having memorized navigation between trap sites. I came to a large fallen tree in my path. It was a big one, extending far in each direction. Fallen trees were common in the forest and I decided just to go over rather than around. Every good biologist knows to step on the log, look over the other side, and then step down. You never step directly over the log in order to avoid stepping on or surprising wildlife that could be on the other side. So, I lifted my leg, and just as I was about to step down on the large tree, directly under my foot was a small copperhead coiled up. I was so worried about what could be on the other side of the log I had not even noticed the little guy sitting right there on top. It was looking straight at my leg. It had not moved yet, relying on its camouflage. It was not aggressive, but I am fairly certain things would've been different had my boot come down on top of that snake.

So, there I stood, one foot in the air with a heavy pack on my back trying to switch momentum. Gravity was not kind to me that day. I lost my balance and had two choices: place my foot next to the snake and risk getting bit, or collapse backwards. I chose the latter; I fell into a pile of leaf litter. After picking myself up and dusting off, I ended up taking many photos of the snake. It remained coiled, having not moved an inch during the whole ordeal. I also ended up picking several ticks off myself from my roll through the leaf litter.

Copperheads weren't the only hazard to look out for in the Ozarks. Timber rattlesnakes were common in the area, and they blended into the forest just as much as—if not better—than the copperheads. I only encountered a few rattlesnakes in my time there, but I'm fairly certain I walked by twice that number without ever noticing.

Cottonmouths, or water moccasins, are another rattleless pit viper found in the area, and they're mostly associated with water. I had a few close encounters with them during my time in the Ozarks, but the closest was while walking along a creek with a coworker. After stopping to say a few words, my coworker looked at me and said, "Scott, you might want to turn around." There, right where I had just walked, was a cottonmouth doing a full display. When it feels threatened, a cottonmouth will gape its mouth and display the white interior, which is how the snake got its name. I have no idea how long the snake had been displaying behind me, but it did cause me to be more watchful that day. I hiked through the dense forest and cross country through brambles and dry leaf piles nearly every day for ten months in the Ozarks. During this time, I encountered dozens of snakes, and none of them chased me or made me feel truly threatened. The few close calls I did have were due to my inattentiveness, not from the snake going out of its way to act aggressive toward me. My only real worry was accidently stepping on one of the camouflaged reptile residents.

***

Besides the venomous snakes, Missouri contained a lot of other unique and interesting wildlife. One of these species was the hognose snake. This medium-sized snake is rear-fanged, and has a very mild venom that's not considered dangerous to humans. What makes this snake truly interesting is that it is the thespian of the snake world. When threatened, the snake will initially try a series of false strikes. If this fails, it will contort the muscles and bones in its face to flatten its head—almost like a cobra—to appear larger than it is. Its last line of defense is to play dead, which the snake does by turning upside down, exposing its tongue and vent, and laying completely motionless, hoping the attacker loses interest.

We found one such hognose one day while herping in our spare time. The snake must have been the William Shatner of the snake community. After putting it in a large bucket so we could measure and later release it, the snake began its death scene. He hissed, flipped over, and began squirming along the edges of the bucket in circles. It continued this display for a solid minute before finally "dying." We then slowly flipped it right side up for pictures. The snake would have none of it. Instead, it insisted on being "dead" and would promptly flip itself back over. After allowing it to be dead for a while it would soon start to slowly turn over and look around. Upon seeing movement from us it would quickly "die" again. Of course, this required another death scene of squirming in circles and then sticking out its tongue. We all couldn't help but laugh at the snake's commitment to the scene. We eventually measured and released the snake, and it always makes me think how elaborate some species survival strategies really are.

***

During my younger days, I was never very good at dealing with some of nature's creatures, no matter how hard I tried. Wasps and hornets gave me the most trouble, and it wouldn't be a field season without at least one wasp incident.

During the initial installation of the drift fences we had to travel refuge roads that had not been traveled in months, possibly years. It was on one such road that I had my first wasp incident in Missouri. I had been wary of them since my encounter at the attic house in California.

We pulled up to a gate on a warm, spring morning. It was one of the last arrays that needed to be installed. It was my turn to open the gate, so I got out of the truck. The truck was a two-door, but had a back seat, where I was sitting. I approached the gate, which was locked with a huge chain. There was no top on the cemented pole that held the gate and it had several holes drilled in it. I pulled out the key and clumsily pulled the chain around the gate for easier access to the lock. The chain made a horrible scraping sound, and the gate rattled and moved under the weight. Suddenly, I heard a buzz, then a whoosh, then a lot more buzzing. I was seeing reddish movement out of the corner of my eye. It was coming out of the pole holding the gate. Wasps! All flying out at once!

I let out an alarm call to warn the others (they called it a scream). I ran, yelling "GO! GO! GO!" toward the truck. I tried the driver door. Locked. I heard more buzzing, so I dove head first into the bed of the truck. This time, I banged on the window screaming, "Go!" There was another word in front of "go" that I will not mention here. This time they went. They drove, mud flew, the truck swayed, and we were gone. Once we stopped, I heard it: the unmistakable sound of uncontrolled laughter. Apparently, my coworkers believed that I had overreacted. My side hurt from where I hit one of the pick axes we had in the bed of the truck. I began to laugh. Maybe my reaction was a bit much. Still, I took every encounter with my

67

nemesis species as a lesson and moved on. I remember thinking, "Wasps, why did it have to be wasps?"

***

Venomous reptiles and stinging insects, while interesting, weren't exactly my favorite encounters. While working in Missouri, I also saw owls, skunks, several species of small mammals, and on one occasion, a newborn deer fawn.

It happened one day while on a recreational hike. A deer with all the white spots and cuteness of Bambi was left in the tall grass near the side of a rarely-used dirt road. I took a quick picture, but after working with deer fawns I knew the risk to its safety if I were to stick around too long.

The only thing I saw cuter than a deer fawn that year was the baby box turtle I found in one of my traps. While the adults grow up to what some people may describe as ugly, no one could dispute the cuteness of the babies. It was only about two inches wide and two inches long. The head was the size of a pencil eraser, and the legs barely stuck out of the shell. The little guy was trying unsuccessfully to climb over a small rock which endeared it to me even more. If there was ever any creature I wanted to keep from my field work, it was that baby turtle. I wanted to, but I knew it would be wrong, so I took my measurements and photos, and then found a nice spot to release it.

***

Life wasn't all fun and adventure in Missouri; there were definitely new obstacles to be found. Before adventuring into the forests or glades of the Ozarks, I had a daily ritual. First, I would put on my jeans and tuck them into my long socks (shorts were never worn). Then, my shirt was tucked into my pants, and I would put on ankle-supporting boots. Permethrin (a strong tick repellent) had been heavily applied to my belt area of my pants and the area around my ankles. I would also thoroughly spray the brim of my hat with insect repellent. Once my clothing was soaked, I would spray my hands and rub my ears with non-DEET repellent. When finished, I would wash my hands to avoid spreading the toxic spray onto any of the animal captures that I might handle during the day. This was all done daily before venturing out to work.

The reason for such elaborate measures were due to two creatures that I had had only brief encounters with until then. Those were ticks and chiggers. While both were equally miserable to run into, their effects were quite different.

Ticks were common in the forest; the thicker the vegetation, the more ticks there were. It was a slow day when we only found three or four of them climbing on our clothes. On a bad day, I believe I counted about 25. And that didn't even include the seed ticks that could number in the hundreds. Seed ticks are essentially baby ticks that are no bigger than the head of a pin. Besides feeding on your blood, the ticks can transfer a variety of diseases through their bite, the most infamous being Lyme disease. After a few months of pulling off ticks and hiking in the forest, I began to actually see them in the brush. They were small (probably only a tenth of an inch long), and would climb to the tops of grasses and ends of branches on shrubs. They would hang from the edge flailing their limbs, hoping to catch onto anything that walked by. I knew they could sense me, as I would often put my hand near them and then move it from side to side. They would follow my hand as it switched directions. As annoying as they were, they could also be fascinating.

Due to the high volume of ticks and the diseases they transferred, daily tick checks had to occur at the end of each day in the field. I always dreaded that part. There's nothing worse than finding one already attached. Often, I would check my pants and find several had bitten into my jeans and were stuck. That was one reason I chose jeans over lighter field pants, even during the summer heat and humidity.

As if ticks weren't enough to deal with, there were also chiggers. These are nearly-invisible, biting mites that leave red, itchy bumps wherever they bite. What made them truly insidious was where there was one bite, there would usually be hundreds more. Entire legs could easily be completely covered from a single walk in tall grass. They didn't venture into the forest much, which helped make our work there a bit easier. The worst encounter I can remember from these cursed arachnids involved my girlfriend. She had to change a tire, or maybe the oil, and was laying on the ground next to the car for nearly half an hour. Though she never felt a bite, the next morning she was covered from shoulder to ankle on one side of her body with red bumps. She looked as if she might have some form of measles. I hurt just looking at her. It was enough to scare me into performing my daily ritual mentioned above.

***

We took a short break during the summer when it got too hot to trap. I eventually returned to work, and found a new ally amongst the creatures of the Ozarks. When I returned to trapping after two months, I was shocked to find large, black and white hornets hanging around every trapping array I came to. At first, I was worried. These huge hornets were at least two inches long, and made a loud buzzing sound when they flew by. I found myself rushing to check my traps between patrols by these insect guardians.

It wasn't long before I saw a pattern to their activity. They would fly up and down the walls of tin leading to the arrays. As I watched them, I soon discovered that they were hunting. Any insect on the ground would be funneled by our traps and make them easy prey to the hornets. After only two months of being gone, the hornets had learned this new hunting behavior. It was amazing. I was still uneasy about their presence until I saw one pick off a yellow jacket and fly away with it. Then it came back and took another. Any species that would take out the smaller, much more aggressive yellow and black hornets was alright by me. From then on, I made my peace with the large bald-faced hornets, as I eventually learned they were called. As long as they were attacking the yellow jackets and not me, I wouldn't mind them hunting near my traps.

***

After a few months on the job, we all realized we could finish checking traps well before the eight hours we were paid for were completed. We didn't feel guilty about this because we all knew it was an eight dollar an hour job at a set rate of 40 hours per week. It didn't matter whether we worked more or less; the pay would be the same. During the days of installing the traps, we worked well over 40 hours a week. We figured this would make up for that extra effort we put in.

However, our short days ended when the rain came in. One morning, after a light rain the night before, I set out for work. I usually left around 8 AM and returned shortly after one in the afternoon. Like most days, I took with me a bag of sunflower seeds and half a gallon of iced tea. I no longer took my lunch with me because I could usually finish before I was hungry again after breakfast. I started toward my traps, excited to see what the rain brought in.

As I hiked to my first of ten trap arrays, I soon became soaked. The rain from the night before clung to every leaf and blade of grass. I was used to the desert where the ground was dry an hour after sunrise. So, my body from the waist down was wet, almost as if I had waded into a stream or river. I soon forgot about my heavily-soaked pants when I saw my first trap. It had been a slow week before the rain; we usually only had three to five captures a day, and most of them had been lizards. I was hoping the rain would change that, and I had just seen a flash of movement in my trap.

I quickly picked up the first trap, and was delighted to find several red-back salamanders and my first slimy salamander. Both are salamanders in the *Plethodontidae* family, which are known as the lungless salamanders. They are called "lungless" because they actually do lack lungs, and instead, use their skin as a respiratory surface to take in oxygen. They are both dark-bodied and small, about two to three inches long, with a short tail. The main difference between the two is that the red-back salamander has a red stripe down its back, and the slimy salamander is covered in white flecks.

After measuring, toe clipping, and releasing the salamanders, I went on to the next trap. It too was filled with the small salamanders. I skipped marking them, and moved on to the other traps. I was beginning to get a bad feeling about the direction of my day. As I suspected, the other traps were teeming with the little amphibians.

That day, I caught nearly 50 slimy salamanders, and had 70 total captures of all species. With each slimy salamander I processed, I learned more about the origin of its name. When threatened, these salamanders secrete a very sticky liquid from their skin. With each salamander I processed, the stickier my hands got. By the tenth slimy salamander, my data sheets were sticking to my hands. By the 50th, the toe clippers were sticking to my hands. It was well after 7 PM when I returned to the house. Except for sunflower seeds, I had not eaten for 12 hours. However, even if I had food I would not have been able to eat it with the residue on my hands. Dirt, sweat, and all manner of forest debris clung to my hands and arms. I was exhausted.

After a shower and dinner, I finally asked the others about their days. My girlfriend had nearly 40 captures and had been out until 4 PM. My roommate had 90 captures and had just barely beat me in. We called that day "The Day of the Salamander," though we all knew that it would likely happen again if we kept getting rain. Hopefully, we would not be caught so off-guard the next time.

***

One of my favorite things about traveling around as a field biologist is exploring new areas. At nearly every job I have worked I have found places to volunteer during my down time; in Missouri it was at Mingo National Wildlife Refuge. This allowed me to explore more wild areas than I would in my normal scope of work. However, even a biologist occasionally needs time off from biology.

While working in Missouri, I had the opportunity to explore St. Louis during a long weekend, which also happened to be the same time as Mardi Gras. The whole crew ended up going. After being cooped up in a wildlife refuge by ourselves, we all needed to escape for a bit. Our first mistake was accepting an invitation to a bar where we were given all-you-can-drink tap beer for free. I am going to disappoint people by not giving all the details of the hijinks that went on that night, but I will say this: at least one of our crew got lost and resorted to bribing a homeless man for directions to the hotel. When that failed, he resorted to paying a pizza-delivery guy for a ride home.

St. Louis wasn't the only trip our crew took together. On St. Patrick's Day, we made a trip to Chicago. I knew I was in trouble when I was woken up at 7 AM to do Irish car bombs with everyone. We were lit by the time we made it to the parade. After several beers—and not one public restroom to be found—some of the crew resorted to the field method of finding a restroom, which was anywhere people couldn't see you directly. Again, I wish I could say more, but I feel those stories are best kept between the crew.

Another memorable trip was our attempt at a lazy canoe ride. We made our plans, and borrowed three canoes for the trip. After packing a fishing rod, food, and several cases of beer, I was ready. What we didn't think about was all the ice and snow pack melting from the horrific ice storms earlier in the year.

We began our trip not noticing the river was several feet higher than in previous years. One of the crew decided to simply float on an inflatable tube. By lunch, a case of beer was gone. By dinner, so was a bottle of Jack Daniel's. We made it to the first camping spot without incident, and stayed there for the night.

The next morning, after recovering from our collective hangover, we began the second leg of the trip, which had a few bends in the river. Nothing serious, we thought. We arrived at the first bend, and the water picked up speed. Suddenly, the people in the first canoe started paddling frantically. Then, on the turn, they tipped over. They did not, however, leave the water.

My canoe was coming next, and suddenly, there were three people wading in chest-high water. None made an effort to leave the area, and canoes are hard to stop, especially in faster moving water. We went wide around them, paddling like crazy. We barely missed my girlfriend, and then had to make the hard turn that had capsized them. We were too wide, the current caught us, and the canoe tipped. Once tipped, the water took hold of our canoe and pinned it to a downed tree. We heard it groan, and watched the metal canoe bend slightly under the pressure.

Luckily, the first canoe was recovered with half of our supplies still intact. After looking at my canoe—pinned and unmovable—we realized how lucky we were. Any one of us could have been pinned between the canoe and the fallen tree. Thankfully, none of us had been drinking the second day.

We all grouped together in the remaining canoes and made our way to the end without incident. We never did get the other canoe out of the river; I still kind of wonder what happened to it. Either way, we made it out unscathed, and it added yet another memorable adventure to my time as a field biologist—one of many I probably never would have experienced had I stayed in Arizona.

***

Towards the end of my time at the refuge, work was becoming routine, and not a lot surprised me anymore. Then, one day, I arrived at one of my farthest-placed traps and found a pile of corn near it.

I didn't know it at the time, but corn is commonly used to bait turkey or deer in Missouri. Baiting too early is illegal and considered akin to poaching. I found this out when I informed the land manager about the discovery and disclosed the location. The man I was talking to was a biologist, but also a former law enforcement officer. He told me that he would keep an eye on it, and for me to report any vehicles I may see in the area.

I left, and that was that. The next few days, I checked my traps as normal, looking out for parked vehicles. I never saw any, which further led to my surprise one morning when I arrived at array #9 and started hiking the trail to my traps. It was on my return trip when I stopped to catch my breath. I was standing in the quiet forest, thinking I was completely alone, when I heard a deep voice say, "Find anything?"

Obviously startled, I jumped, spun in a circle, and looked around. Nothing. I spun again, and this time, I saw a bit of movement. The leaves on the ground began to move, and a person seemed to materialize from them. There, laying on the ground near the corn dump site, was the land manager, in full guile suit, holding a shotgun. He had been waiting to catch the poachers when they returned. How long he had been doing this, I had no idea. It's a very unnerving thing to think you're alone, only to suddenly find out you're not—even more so when the person surprising you is holding a gun. Once I caught my breath, I began to wonder how many days he had been hidden there, watching me come and go. I also became very thankful that I had not chosen to relieve myself in this area of the trail; things could have gotten truly awkward between us.

***

One random thing I am proud of—and I have no idea why— is that I have actually swung on a vine. During the initial installation of the drift fence arrays, we often had to cut through roots, and occasionally, vines. On one such occasion, we were near a small ravine, and a particularly large tree was nearby. It had a grape vine hanging from it, directly in the way of our trap. After cutting through the four inch diameter vine my coworker gave it a pull. It held. Then he lifted himself on it. Again, it held. The next thing we all saw was him running and swinging over the ravine on the vine and coming back. We all sat staring, then, almost in unison, the three of us jumped up claiming next.

We spent the next thirty minutes taking turns swinging and taking pictures. On one of my turns, I ran, jumped with the vine, and swung to the tree across the ravine. For reasons that still eludes me to this day, I reached out and grabbed ahold of the tree. Upon doing so, I lost grip of the vine and it fell away. Now I was 20 feet above ground, hugging a tree for dear life. I sat there for a few and then tried to shimmy down. I started wiggling and inching my way down. Then, I felt the bark slip, and then break, which sent me plummeting into the leaf litter below.

When I hit the ground, I thought I cracked a rib. It had knocked the wind out of me, and I sat for about ten minutes while the pain subsided and I caught my breath. I was only bruised—both my ribs and my pride, but it was still fun.

***

While working in the wildlife field, you are required to learn more than just biology. Due to limited funding (for a variety of reasons), conservation biology is always struggling with budgets. When something breaks during nonprofit or government work, you cannot simply get it repaired or install a new one, either because of the remote location or the cost.

Sometimes, wildlife biologists also need to be mechanics, groundskeepers, computer technicians, electricians, and anything else the projects need. I have installed fences, fixed computers, installed video and trail cameras, operated and repaired all manner of machines, and built trails. In Missouri, I became a lumberjack.

During the summer, I had been tasked with invasive plant removal while it was too hot to trap reptiles. One of the projects the ranch had in mind was removing tulip poplars. These were 50 to 170-foot-tall trees that were planted years ago, and were spreading to unwanted areas of the ranch.

While in the training period, I was given a six hour training course on how to use a chainsaw, and most of what I cut were trees that had already fallen. In fact, the largest tree I had taken down myself was only ten feet tall and pretty thin. I arrived at the site of the trees that were to be removed and looked up. They towered above me. I was intimidated. I had no supervision and only a partner that had missed the training to assist me.

I remember the first few trees went quick, but then I tried one of the larger trees. I cut my notch and then began to saw. I may have misjudged the trees lean, or the wind had caught it. The tree leaned and pinched my saw. It was stuck. I had already cut more than half way through. I heard cracking. The tree was going to fall! I did not know which way the tree was going to fall but I did know which way it was not going to fall—the way I had intended. I abandoned the saw and ran forward, and my partner followed. The tree fell and made a thunderous boom. Then we laughed. It was probably the adrenaline, but we found the intense situation humorous.

I wish I could say that was the only tree we ran from that summer. Eventually, I got the hang of things and really enjoyed it. I always enjoyed learning skills they never taught me in college.

***

It was almost winter again when it was finally time to leave Missouri. The herps were no longer moving, and the weather was starting to turn cold. I was missing the desert, but I had made such good friends at this job and learned so much that I was hesitant to leave. We had one final party on Halloween, and then parted ways the next day.

Like all the jobs before, I was sad to see my friends go. We all joked about a reunion and meeting up for some herping, but I knew it was unlikely. I would have like to have stuck around and had a few more days with the people I had lived and worked with for the last ten months, but I had a job interview back in Arizona; it seemed likely that I was going to be working with Arizona Game and Fish again.

The drive back was rushed. I had only two days to get home in time for my job interview. The drive back was also strained. My girlfriend had not lined up a job, or even an interview. She was headed back to her parents' home in California, and I was headed to Arizona. We rarely spoke of how this would affect our relationship, other than to say it was only a few hours' drive to see each other. We said that, but we both knew what this probably meant for us. We had been together for nearly two years by then, and had lived and worked together for much of it.

We arrived in Arizona and then went our separate ways. We visited each other during for the first couple months, but by the time New Year's rolled around, I was single again.

1. Jones Center Cabin: Newton, GA

2. Main House: Orange County, CA

3. Housing Trailers: Winona, MO

4. Bunk House: Roosevelt Lake, AZ

6. Improvised Hat. Military Range, AZ

7. Collaring Deer Fawn: Roosevelt Lake, AZ

8. Swinging on a Vine: Winona, MO

18. Mining hotel: Near Kingman, AZ

9. Water Dragon: Brisbane, Australia

10. Speckled Rattle Snake: Clark County, NV

11. Skink Not Cooperating: Winona, MO

12. Baby Box Turtle: Winona, MO

13. Eastern Diamond Back: Newton, GA

14. Alligator Snapping Turtle: Newton, GA

15. Barking Tree Frog: Newton, GA

17. Random things I found in the desert:

6 Desert Life (Part One)

Sometimes, a person follows their passion and works hard at it, which eventually leads to a career. However, a lot of the time, it seems like a person simply falls into something along the way that then becomes a career. This is what happened to me. After moving from town to town and working with all manner of wildlife, I began working with an animal that would dominate my professional life for the next half decade: the desert tortoise.

After Missouri, my life did not go as planned. I did not get the full-time, permanent agency job that I was hoping for, I was back living with my parents, and my girlfriend had just left me. It was also the first time I started wanting a more permanent home. For the last three years, I had loved wandering the country and being a nomad. It was nice not being tied down, but then something changed when I returned to Arizona. Deep down, I always knew the Sonoran Desert was my home. I just hadn't realized it until I saw the first saguaro-covered hills on my drive back. I wanted to stay there. It's not that I didn't want to travel more; I just wanted a place to leave from and come back to. With this in mind, I took my third job working for Arizona Game and Fish. This time, it was for a year, but I had ideas to try and convince them to make it permanent.

The job was surveying for desert tortoises. I was part of the research branch of Arizona Game and Fish. The job sounded great—hiking all over the state, camping, and finding all kinds of wildlife along the way. Then, I talked to some of my old friends from the flycatcher project (they had hung around the department and now were full-time employees). All I kept hearing from them was how hard the surveys were and how hot it was. I didn't listen. After all, I had twice survived Roosevelt Lake, and besides, this would be my third job with the department, so surely they would give me a full-time, permanent position this time, right?

***

The job started like all the others with GPS and compass training. ATV training was fun, and although I would like to have taken it again, I was excused from the off-road training this time around.

Then, they brought in the tortoises. Until this job, I had never worked much with the desert tortoise. They're definitely funny creatures, and the more I learned, the funnier they became. They are oval reptiles with a shell, elephantine limbs, scaled front limbs used to protect its face, and a funny-looking head that stretches out with a bird-like beak on the end. They are grey to green in color, and are usually found covered with dirt, which helps them blend in with their desert surroundings remarkably well. Tortoises spend most of their lives in half-moon-shaped burrows or caves made of caliche (sedimentary rock that's like a natural cement). They emerge to eat and drink in the spring and after the monsoon rains in the summer, and to breed whenever conditions are favorable.

After a week of training, the three new techs were sent to the field under the leadership of a crew leader and an experienced technician, both of whom had worked on the project the previous year. The funny thing I noticed was that every crew I was on before I broke up with my girlfriend had at least an equal number of girls to guys, but after we broke up, all my crews seemed to be mostly guys.

The three new techs were myself, a marine who went back to

Scott Lillie

school for his wildlife degree, and a former marine biologist who
ended up in the desert to help his wife. It was an interesting crew.

My new home was a cot—no tent or pickup truck to sleep in.
It was more convenient that way, since we moved camp every day.
There was no home base—we drove, worked, camped, and then
packed up and started at a new site the next day.

While difficult, moving camp each day gave me the
opportunity to see much of the back country in Arizona that I had
never seen before, and never would have seen otherwise. Old mining
camps hidden away in the mountains, valleys only accessible after a
two hour drive on a dirt road, and mountains that most people would
think are unhikable, with amazing views from the top.

Camp life was more difficult this time around. We worked
year-round in the deserts, and by June the heat was in full force. We
hiked steep, rocky, desert mountains 8-10 hours a day in 110-degree
heat, only to end the day with a multi-hour trip driving down a dirt
road, and then trying to cool down and sleep outside when it was still
90 degrees. We cooked by gas grill or by campfire. Our food was
kept in ice chests stored in the backs of the trucks. Our schedule was
eight days of camping in the field followed by six wonderful days off.

This was the first job I had ever truly doubted whether I was
capable of doing it. The first day, we hiked until my legs were shaking
and my feet ached, and that was before we even started our surveys.
The survey areas included a lot of wilderness areas with limited road
access—hiking five miles just to get to the survey area was not
unheard of. This was also how my first day began.

In the beginning, it took all of my mental and physical
strength just to get out of the truck. For a while, I would just stare at
the mountains we were supposed to climb. Then, I would get out of
the truck, feel my sore legs, and wonder if I could make it. Somehow,
I always did. In the end, I was always glad I decided to get out of the
truck. The views were amazing, there was always plenty of wildlife to
photograph, and it was a good feeling to push myself beyond what I
thought were my limits. However, when I woke up the next morning,
the battle would begin all over again.

***

By the end of the first month, I ended each day the same way.

I cooked, drank a beer or two, took ibuprofen for my sore legs, and then slept. I was too exhausted to do anything else. There was no after-work exploring, and no herping at night. Some days, I was too tired to even cook canned food.

One day, after a long day of hiking, we were all talking by the camp fire. It was dark by then, and we had all put in nearly 13 hours that day. I somehow managed to open my can of chili and get it in the pot without collapsing. I was almost as hungry as I was tired. Almost.

When the chili finally started boiling I took it off the fire. I was eating straight from my cooking pot. The first bite tasted amazing—everything tasted good when you were that hungry. I was listening to a story and stirring my pot when suddenly a moth as a big as a half-dollar flew straight into my chili. When I flinched, the chili sloshed back and forth, and the moth was lost.

I looked up and saw one of the techs looking at me. The question was evident on his face: "Well, are you going to eat it?" I looked back at my chili. I still couldn't see the moth, but there was no doubt it was in there. I was hungry and tired. I grabbed my spoon and took a bite. A few minutes later I was done with the entire pot. Truthfully, I never really tasted or felt anything other than chili. I remember thinking how much things had changed since I had started college. I never would have eaten a bowl of chili with a moth in it before. Maybe I would make it as a field biologist after all.

***

For safety reasons, we always traveled in pairs in the desert. There were mountain lions, rattlesnakes, steep terrain, cactus, and of course, people. I liked all of the crew by the end of the season, but in the beginning the two new technicians were my favorite to work with.

RR was a marine who later got his degree and became a biologist. When he arrived on the crew it was his first paid wildlife job, but his military training gave him a distinct advantage. Usually, it takes a few seasons to learn the tricks to navigating all types of terrain, driving (correctly) off-road, and hiking in the desert terrain. He was familiar with all of it, having been a veteran of the war in Iraq. He was fresh out of college, and the biology side of things was still fresh in his mind. So while it was his first real wildlife job, I did not consider him to be a newbie by any stretch.

On this particular day in late spring, RR was with me and we were surveying a flat wash. It had been an easier day, and I was truly enjoying myself. We were over two-thirds of the way done and had seen several snakes so far. RR was ahead of me, pulling down old flagging from our survey. I was poking around some bushes looking for lizards and snakes.

Suddenly, I heard a yell. Startled, I looked up. RR was not one to scare easily, so when I saw him running full speed towards me yelling, "GO!" I didn't hesitate to start running, as well.

Within a few seconds he had passed me—running was not my strong suit—and all kinds of scenarios were going through my head. During training, we had been told of illegal immigrants using the desert to smuggle drugs, so perhaps he stumbled on a drug exchange. Meth houses were also popular in uninhabited parts of Arizona, so maybe we were running from meth dealers.

Finally, he slowed, then stopped. "What?" I asked emphatically.

"Look!" he said, thrusting his binoculars at me. Still not understanding, I took them, and looked. At first, I saw nothing, but then saw something that seemed odd. Initially, it looked like a shadow. I focused the binos, and finally saw what he was running from: thousands, probably tens of thousands of bees, flying at what would have been the end of our survey.

We watched them. This was not a passing swarm; they seemed to be hovering over something. We wisely decided not to investigate, and instead, left the area. The survey was completed in our minds.

My next encounter with bees was late in the summer. The monsoons had just started, and it was probably the most miserable time for day surveys. The storms didn't come in until the afternoon when our surveys were already completed, and they usually went around our area, anyway. I remember being on the side of a barren mountain and recording the temperature at 117 degrees F, with 40 percent humidity. I have worked in the humidity of Missouri and Georgia, and the desert heat of Nevada and California, but nothing has been as miserable as that day.

My clothes were drenched with sweat. It looked as if I had walked out of a swimming pool wearing my clothes. I dropped down into a wash at the base of the mountain when I scared up a jackrabbit, which was not uncommon.

This jackrabbit was having as bad of day as I was. It popped out of a creosote bush only a foot or so in front of me, and I jumped back, almost as startled as the rabbit. It took off running and ran straight into a large caliche cave. I stood catching my breath when it darted back out of the cave. Before I had much of a chance to think, I heard it: buzzing. Then, I immediately noticed the rabbit had something on it. My first thought was dirt from the cave, but then I saw them: bees.

The rabbit was covered in hundreds of bees, and many more were emerging from the cave. Bees were mostly dormant at that time of day, and they just happened to all be in the cave that the unlucky rabbit chose to seek shelter in. When they started to emerge I did not wait to see what happened next. The rabbit went north, I ran south. I ran until I was out of breath, which didn't take long carrying a pack and wearing hiking boots. I looked back. No bees. I took out my map and crossed out that part of the survey. I never saw the rabbit again.

I was not stung that day, and I consider myself lucky for having never stuck my head into a cave of bees when looking for burrowed tortoises. I had always been cautious of sticking my head in caves in fear of snakes, but now I had something else to be wary of.

***

I had learned that the Sonoran Desert hid many large hives of bees, and sometimes, they find you before you find them.

In southern Arizona, there can be a lot of desert pavement, which is basically ground made up of small rocks and soil compacted tightly together. These areas rarely have trees, and are not great places to camp in the desert. One day we were surrounded by miles of desert pavement and steep mountains. When we finally found a decent camping spot—a wash lined with small Palo Verde and mesquite trees—we chose to stay in it for most of the week.

The first night, we had visitors: a few bees that annoyed us and drank from the water that drained from the coolers and the water left over from our dishes.

The next night they brought friends. We had arrived earlier that day and set up camp in the daylight. The first of the bees arrived about an hour before sunset. Ten minutes later, every water source we had was covered. Our drinking cooler looked like it had a beard of bees on it starting at the water spout. We could not even open a water bottle without bees swarming. We had to put our chairs and cots several hundred feet from the coolers and any water. This lasted until a few minutes after sunset when the bees disappeared.

From then on, if we were in that area we had to do our cleaning and drinking prior to an hour before sunset, otherwise known as "The Bee Hour."

***

Working in southern Arizona had more challenges than just bees. We were working near the Mexican border, and during this time there was a high amount of drug smuggling and violence on the other side of the border. Many agency personnel had been targets of border violence. For our protection, we were asked not to wear any clothing with the state symbol on it, so as not to appear to be associated with any law enforcement agency.

While working on the border, I really appreciated the U.S. Border Patrol's presence and commitment, but it also could be an obstacle with our work. Often, we would ride quads through extremely dusty areas while heading to our field sites. One day, after I had been camping for six days—and had not taken more than a field shower the whole time—I was riding one of the quads to the field site. I was going full throttle. I finally slowed to look at my GPS when I saw the truck. I was being followed. They must have seen the dust trail and came to investigate. I was surprised they could keep up with me in their trucks. I waited for the dust to clear, and then saw the Border Patrol emblem.

I reached for my wallet, and then panicked. I had no wallet and no ID. I must have left it in the truck. I was wearing my field clothes that looked more like a vagrant's clothing than a state employee's. I was less than a mile from the border, caked in days of dirt. "This could be bad," I thought. "I am going to a holding cell."

The officer walked up to me and asked what I was doing. As soon as I mentioned I had no ID he started having an attitude. I don't think he liked my lack of ID or my clothing. I explained the situation and he looked doubtful, but luckily, my partner eventually pulled up, and he had his state ID badge. The officer then told us there was activity spotted in the area, and to be careful. He actually lightened up a lot, and after talking for a while, he explained a lot of smugglers are using quads. They roll carpet on the tires so the tracks they leave look much older than they are. "Creative," I thought. He then wished us luck and went on his way.

Sadly, that wasn't the only encounter with Border Patrol that summer. We camped at different spots every day, and really didn't know where we would end up stopping. This made it hard to keep them informed of our exact location, except for on the live ranges. On those areas, everyone knew our every move for good reason.

When camping off the range, it was a good idea to call in your location to all law enforcement agencies in the area. However, with limited service, it usually seemed like a pain. Often, it just wasn't practical to call, seeing that it was over an hour drive to cell service, and we had already worked 10-12 hours. However, we did learn why it was such a good idea one night in May.

It had been a long, hot field day, and we were beat. We didn't even really try to find shade, since the area seemed flat and treeless all around us. We hit our cots as soon as the sun went down. I was asleep early that night. Then it hit us. Two trucks rolling in from either side, their revving engines waking me from a dead sleep. Spot lights hit our camp. Then they panned over to the vehicles emblazoned with the Arizona Game and Fish logo. After that, the lights went off. Then, after a few moments, the trucks pulled away. No words were spoken, and we were left in darkness. It was obviously the Border Patrol. They must have spotted our camp and thought illegal activity was occurring.

***

Camino Del Diablo—that was the name of the road we were taking to our work site one day. The name roughly translates to "The Devil's Highway." There is actually a book about it, and I heard somewhere that over 700 people have died on this road since it was built in the late 1800s. There is no water and little shade. This was where we were working for the week.

The air temperature was over 117 degrees, and the ground temperature was over 130. We were down there because of an old report of a wildlife manager seeing a tortoise in the area. The area was being managed by one of the armed services now. We were doubtful at best that there were tortoises in the area, but it would not be a complete study if we did not investigate.

After three grueling days, we finally called it quits. We hadn't see any tortoises; in fact, we barely saw anything alive at all. We hadn't even any tortoise sign; no scat, tracks or carcasses. Nothing walked around that area during the day besides stupid humans like us. That's how I felt—stupid. Every other desert creature knew not to be out, but here I was walking at noon, in June, next to The Devil's Highway. This is the type of thing most people don't think about when the word "biologist" is mentioned. However, with this job you take the good with the bad.

***

Performing biological surveys on an active military base comes with a whole list of new obstacles. You have to coordinate with the military, get clearance cards, and then clear any pictures taken on the base. One of the last weeks of summer we had moved to a very active training area.

The first day, I knew these were going to be interesting surveys. We were walking a transect with a torn-up building to our right. It looked like a movie prop. Halfway through the transect, a group of Humvees pull up from a dirt road about 30 feet from us. Uniformed soldiers burst from all the jeeps and began taking positions aiming at the building. A flurry of action happened at once. People running for the building, commands being yelled, and people moving from jeep to jeep. Then, as quick as it began, the Humvees were loaded up and the armored jeeps pulled out in a cloud of dust. I imagined we looked like cartoon characters standing there in the dust, jaws dropped. It was intense. Then, we were walking again. After that, I started keeping an eye out not just for tortoises on those surveys.

***

I worked on a variety of military ranges during that year with the department. From aerial bombing ranges to sniper fields, we surveyed all of it. Sometimes, we were only given a window of a few hours to get in and out before the bombing would start again. They would start with a call at three in the morning to tell us we had until 10 AM to get a particular area surveyed and get out. We would then grab our gear and drive like crazy to get there, and I was always afraid of engine trouble or a flat tire. I didn't exactly enjoy being an on-call biologist, but I understood that military training always took precedence.

The scariest day I had involved miscommunication. This time, I wasn't working with the crew leader, but one of the new techs. We were given our plot coordinates and were driving towards them when we ran into a road block.

After calling the field leader and confirming that we were on the correct road, we went around the barrier. Things were fine until we came to another barrier. Again, we called the lead, and again we were told to go around the barrier. After going around that road block, we came to a third "road closed" sign. Thinking that they really wanted this road closed, we called again. Our leader said that he had confirmed that our location was good and to keep going, so we pressed on.

Our plot was in a creosote flat. The only thing that broke the plot up was a large wash that ran from corner to corner. Upon reaching the wash we saw a few vehicles lining up in the distance. We thought it was strange, but continued the survey. A few minutes later, a tank emerged on the southern end of our plot, with our vehicle to the northwest. Now we were getting worried, but kept going while keeping a wary eye on the tank. Then, it raised it cannon and pointed north—it was not directly over our heads but seemed close enough. At this point, we decided we were done, and started to walk back. Then…BOOM! The cannon roared. It was deafening in the otherwise still desert. I did a full superman dive in the wash on pure reflex. You could feel the vibrations in your bones. I honestly could not imagine facing anything like that on a battlefield. I pulled myself out of the bushes I had dove into and we ran to the truck. Looking back, I am sure it was just some guys having a little fun with us, but it was still an intense moment. I often tell a slightly exaggerated story of how I was almost shot by a tank.

Working on military ranges definitely gave me a new

perspective on the intense training that our armed forces go through. Just trying to survey on an active military range was intense enough for me. I can't imagine what it must be like to actually have people shooting at you on a real battlefield.

***

So, the season went on. We would find tortoises, put transmitters on them, and then track their movements. By the time the monsoons arrived, I had felt that I had seen everything there was to see out there. Even the hiking didn't seem that bad anymore, as I had been able to work myself into pretty good shape over the last few months.

One hot and humid day, I was near Yuma on some pretty barren terrain. Sparse vegetation covered the area, and jagged mountains stuck out in the distance. Then, we came to a solid rock shelf with a little bit of water on it.

There, surrounded by burning hot rock and dry soil was a bit of water, and in that water were hundreds of tadpoles. It was the only water for miles, and it was shaded by a large boulder. After looking for a bit, we found another surprise. Cramming into a crack at the edge of the puddle were hundreds of fully-formed toads. They were all trying to burrow into the crack before the water dried up. This area is one of the hottest and driest spots in the country, and we couldn't believe there was aquatic life living there. That particular puddle probably only exists for one week out of the year, and yet, there they were, hundreds of toads.

I always think of that scene and others whenever I hear plans for solar and wind farms in the desert. Most of the voices come from people who have no real idea of the amount and uniqueness of life that can exist in some of the harshest deserts. One small change to the environment, and this entire population of toads would not have existed. This is a lesson I will always carry with me.

***

I should say that the desert was not all challenging; it definitely had its finer moments. During my time there, I saw over a hundred sunrises and sunsets. I saw them rise from behind the mountains, creating all manner of reds, yellows, and purples. I saw the sunset over the Colorado River, slowly illuminating the flowing water. I saw the sun peak out of the monsoon clouds, creating rainbows that contrasted with the stark desert landscape.

I also saw an incredible amount of wildlife. From tortoises and snakes to the cat-like kit foxes, I saw everything the desert had to offer that year. I was again privileged to see the desert bighorn sheep. I saw coyotes, lizards, and owls. I also saw hawks of all sorts, from the migrants just passing through to the year-round desert residents. I saw many bobcats and skunks, and stumbled upon the clumsy javelina rooting in a wash, their smell giving them away. The only thing I did not see that year was a mountain lion; that would have completed my season.

***

After being in a relationship for several years, and followed by a few months of the single life, I was trying to get back into dating. At first, I thought it would be easy since every crew usually had a few single girls on it. However, it was proving to be more difficult on this job than I remembered.

I was finding that dating a girl and trying to explain to her that I could only see her every other week was difficult. Most girls thought it was fine at first, but soon became disillusioned. After a few weeks, it usually became more of a hassle than it was worth. Other times, I simply needed to get something done on my weekend off, which meant I wouldn't see a particular girl for four weeks—this usually did not go well either.

Soon, I all but gave up dating, and started devoting my time to volunteering on any conservation project I could find. I worked on barbed wire removal, invasive plant removal, invasive frog removal, and even volunteered on more tortoise surveys. It was on a bullfrog removal project when I realized for the first time—but not the last—how dangerous conservation work can be.

We were netting large amounts of invasive bullfrogs and tadpoles in southeastern Arizona near the Mexico border. There were just two of us, and we had planned on camping that night. We had already worked past sunset, and were headed back to camp for a break when, suddenly, the crew leader's cell phone started going off.

It was message after message and missed call after missed call. When she looked at the text she looked up and said, "We are leaving NOW!"

We were flying down the dirt roads at night toward our camp while she explained the situation. A wildlife manager and a Bureau of Land Management officer were shot at—and one of them wounded—by suspected drug smugglers a few hours earlier. The biggest shock was that it happened less than a mile from our camp, and the men responsible were last seen heading our way.

We pulled into camp, frantically threw our belongings in our cars, and headed out. It wasn't until I was out of the canyon and off the dirt roads that I felt safe. It was late by the time we were on the Highway, and past 3 AM when I arrived home. I was thankful things had not gotten worse, and the wildlife manager who was shot turned out to be okay. After that, I became extra cautious when hiking in southern Arizona, and started to carry my own firearm when not working for the state.

***

By the end of the season, I was tired. I missed having a regular schedule. I missed having a relationship. I missed seeing my friends and family on a regular basis. I was burnt out. I guess that happens to most field biologists at some point.

After the season was over, I tried to leave the biology field. I took a job at a hospital, and planned on having a normal life again. The problem was that I hadn't had a normal life in so long, and had pretty much forgotten what it was like. Sure it was easy—no hiking in the heat or in the snow, no bugs in your food or bees stealing your water, no worries about animal attacks or drug smugglers shooting at you, and also no tanks, jets, or border patrol. However, for me this also meant no excitement. After a while, I started to miss all of it. I missed knowing that on any day I could see a mountain lion, or have lunch at the top of a mountain. I missed the sunrises and sunsets. I missed the stars and campfires. So after just a few short months living the normal life, I was on the road to my next field job. I was headed to Las Vegas to work with the federally-threatened Mohave desert tortoise. On my drive, I was thinking "Camping, field work, and Las Vegas—this could be trouble."

7 Desert Life (Part Two)

I arrived in Las Vegas, Nevada, only a day before my new job started. I was told I would be sharing a house with my crew. This would be interesting, considering we had a crew of 15 people.

I pulled up to an average-sized home in an average neighborhood in Las Vegas. It was three bedrooms—one for the girls, one for the guys, and a small bedroom for the only couple on the project. The first person I met was a young guy named Colt who had arrived with his mom and grandma. He later became my field partner.

All but one of the crew had arrived by nightfall. All the guys piled into the bedroom. One by one, they took the sofa bed, the sleeper bed, and the twin. One guy set up his bedroll on the floor. This left a king-sized bed for me and the last member of the crew, who had yet to arrive. I settled in the king bed and huddled onto one side, leaving lots of room for the new guy on the oversized mattress. When I awoke the next morning, I was alone in the bed.

The last guy to arrive came in the room and saw the king bed, but elected to sleep on the living room floor. He said he would rather not start a new job by climbing into bed with a strange guy in the middle of the night. I couldn't help but laugh. In the back of my mind I had hoped that would be the case. I then had a king bed for two more nights by myself before the other crew members objected.

***

When I first met Colt, he seemed kind of odd—after all, none of the biologists I had worked with before had showed up on the first day with their parents. Then, I found out his story. He had left a well-paying job doing computer GIS work, and traveled to Costa Rica to volunteer working with sea turtles. He just gave up his old life and decided to try something new. I always respected him for that. That being said, his inexperience definitely showed early on. He rarely set up his tent while camping, usually electing to sleep in the cab of the truck, even though he was over 6'2" tall. I would see him in the fetal position trying to sleep, then I would sprawl out in the bed of our pickup truck as comfortable as can be.

Colt knew little about the desert, or life in the field. However, he seemed to adapt quickly. We also got along great, and he really was the best possible partner for me. He was friendly, and always ready to grab a beer and hang out. We talked sports and told stories from our past. I helped him learn to identify the herps of the desert, and also gave some pointers on field life.

After a day or two in the field, we would need to fill up on gas, which we tried to time with dinner. Unfortunately, that usually meant fast food, sodas, and beer—my diet was reverting back to what it was on my first field season. Our preferred gas station had a Bowlingo game and sold pitchers of beer for two dollars. We ended up killing many hot desert afternoons there.

Colt and I quickly became good friends. This was fortunate, because at this job you were in the field all week with your partner. You rarely saw anyone else at the remote sites, and camped in new locations every day. We were together five days a week for three months eating, camping, and working—no breaks. If we didn't get along, I could see one of us getting "lost" in the desert and not making it back.

***

This project involved line distance sampling for the federally-threatened Mohave desert tortoise at sites in both Nevada and California. It was overseen by the United States Fish and Wildlife Service, which is required to take actions to return threatened or endangered wildlife to healthy populations, or at least stop the decline. Line distance sampling is a method that they use to check population levels. However, it wasn't a survey method that I was used to. It involved walking with a partner who was 20 meters behind you and looking for tortoises, all while trying to stay on a straight line or bearing. After three kilometers, you turn, and eventually make a square. The idea is to only count what you see; the person walking behind is supposed to catch anything you might miss. While this is happening, the telemetry people are tracking tortoises all day, multiple times a day, to record what percentage of tortoises with transmitters are above ground and what percentage are below. Then, using those percentages you adjust the actual number found with how many are out there.

To simplify, let's say there are ten tortoises equipped with transmitters, with eight above ground. That means eighty percent of tortoises in that area should be above ground. So, if the survey team found four tortoises, you would add the 20 percent that you assume are still underground and out of view of the survey teams.

The point is, we had to walk a straight line—like with my willow flycatcher surveys a few years ago—no matter how difficult the terrain was. We walked 12 kilometers a day through rugged mountains and deep washes, and once surveyed through a football field-sized area of jumping cholla. I was coming to find out that all tortoise work was challenging, to say the least.

***

The first week of surveys went well for us. Colt and I were sent out to the California sites, and found four tortoises. We also found mating sidewinder rattlesnakes, mating tortoises, and mating horned lizards (the horny toads were living up to their nickname). It was a good week for us.

We had found out during a check-in that no other group had

found a tortoise. That was also the evening we observed a tortoise walking across the road while we cooked dinner. I remember telling the other crews about that and hearing their outburst: "We walked all week and found none and you guys found four! Hell, there are so many where you are that they walk up to you at camp!"

The next week we were sent to the Nevada sites and found out why no one found any tortoises that week. The temperatures had dropped far below normal, and at one point we were being snowed on (not a lot of tortoises are found in the snow). I am not a fan of the cold—especially when working with cold blooded species that you do not find in the cold—but I knew it wouldn't be long before it would warm up and we would get back to finding interesting animals. Nine months earlier, I had been thinking about how bad it was surveying in the heat, and now I was complaining about surveying in the snow. I was definitely being what's known as a "fair-weather biologist." I did not want to become one of those, so I shut my mouth, and kept surveying.

***

By the time we finished the first week of surveys, we had moved to a new field house. Monday through Friday we camped out in the desert, and on the weekends we stayed in a three bedroom house—15 people in a three bedroom house! And one of the bedrooms was an office. I had picked a nice patch of floor behind a table as my spot, but luckily, I was driving back to Phoenix most weekends to help prepare for my brother's wedding. This kept me from sleeping on the floor, and kept me out of trouble in Las Vegas.

***

During the first few weeks of surveys, the weather was colder than normal at the northern sites, especially at night and in the mornings. Often, the temperature would be close to freezing—something not many people think of when they think of the desert. The temperature can actually fluctuate by 50 degrees in a single day.

One night, we had set up camp off a major highway. It was nighttime, and we had already eaten. We were listening to the radio and watching the highway. There was a cop flashing its lights on the side of the road. While watching the flashing lights, we saw a motorcycle switch lanes and turn off the highway onto an old dirt road—our old dirt road.

The motorcycle started down the road toward us. I didn't like random encounters in the desert; too many weirdoes' out there. Although, I wondered how many people thought the same about me when traveling through the desert.

As the motorcycle was coming up our road, it turned off its light. I listened, and it came close to our camp site and stopped. Then there was just silence. Whoever it was, they were close, and it just seemed weird to me. I got a bad vibe.

After a small debate with Colt, we decided to move camp. We haphazardly packed everything up, and took off down the bumpy dirt road. I left my sleeping bag sprawled out on the bed of the truck because I was too lazy to set it up again. We found a new site and parked the truck.

I was just about to climb into bed when I felt it: my sleeping bag was wet. Not just a little, but soaked. Our water jug had spilled during the ride. A cool breeze sent a chill through me, and I knew I was in for a long night.

I ended up sleeping in the truck that night. I wore nearly every piece of clothing I brought, clean or dirty. I did not bring much heavier clothing because it usually warmed up at first light, and my sleeping bag was very warm. It froze that night, as did I. The windows had a thick layer of frost, and my sleeping bag I had hung to dry was frozen stiff.

Needless to say, I did not sleep that night. I knew I could not run the car because we would need the gas to drive out on the dirt roads the next day. So, there I sat, teeth chattering, counting the hours until sunrise while Colt snored in the back seat.

***

Sometimes, I forget how I must appear to others after having spent a long time in the field. One night, we were driving back from a survey plot and saw a truck parked on the side of the road. I immediately recognized it as the vehicle of another nonprofit group doing wildlife work in the area. I saw a couple girls leaning over something on the side of the road at sunset. I quickly deduced that it must be a snake or lizard that they had found on the road.

I turned to Colt and told him what I thought. "Let's go see what they got!" I said excitedly. He quickly agreed, as we had not seen a snake all week. I swerved to the side of the road, and we jumped out and quickly walked to the two girls leaning over what was sure to be a snake.

The girls looked up, and suddenly, it hit me what they were probably thinking as two large, disheveled guys ran toward them after their strange, unmarked truck swerved off to the side of the otherwise deserted road. We were dressed in ragged clothes and both sporting unkempt beards. They were clearly beyond nervous.

I quickly blurted out, "We're biologists!" thinking that would put them at ease. It did a little. Once we explained we were on the tortoise project, they smiled (the tortoise project was kind of famous in the area).

After chatting a moment, we found out—to our disappointment—that they were photographing a lupine flower, not a snake. We returned to our truck and continued to our next site. On the drive back, I glanced at my partner, the 6'2" guy with a scraggly beard and disheveled clothes. I decided that if I did not know him, I too would be nervous if he came running at me on a desert road.

***

As we got closer to the end of the season, everything had become routine. I barely thought about sleeping in the back of the truck, or cooking over a camp stove. It was normal to pack up every morning and move on. It had been my life for over a year and a half—moving to a new location every day and walking our survey line looking for wildlife. However, when doing wildlife surveys you can't let things get too routine.

It was a sunny day and we were hiking up a mountain made up of black volcanic rock. It was rugged, and sure footing was hard to come by. I couldn't really picture tortoises climbing this stuff, but they had surprised me before. I think I was in the middle of that thought when Colt—who was walking behind me—gave a yell.

I immediately thought that I had missed a tortoise. I hurried back to where he was standing. There, right in the middle of the line—the same line I had just walked—was a huge speckled rattlesnake. I must have stepped next to it, if not right over it. It stayed still until we lingered a bit too long, at which point it gave a rattle. I could not believe I had missed it. Things could have been bad, since we were nowhere near our truck or even a road. I began to wonder how many venomous snakes I had walked past and never even noticed.

***

On one of my last days looking for tortoises, I was riding with another surveyor when we saw a tortoise in the road. We had moved to the translocation site, so tortoises were much more common. We were about 40 meters away, and I was driving less than ten miles per hour.

"Tortoise" he said. "Yeah" I replied. I kept driving. I wanted to get closer to take a look. "TORTOISE" he said louder and with more urgency. "I see it" I said. I slowed, but kept going. "TORTOISE!" he yelled and pointed ahead. Something in his voice told me something was wrong. I slammed on the breaks and skidded to a halt.

There, right in the tire ruts, was a small juvenile tortoise. This was not the tortoise I had seen. I was paying so much attention to the adult tortoise crossing the road ahead of me that I had completely zoned out and missed the little guy right in front of me. I—a biologist—had almost ran over a federally-threatened species. It was certainly a humbling experience, and taught me never become too complacent in the field.

***

I had spent three months camping out, seeing mountains and springs from Las Vegas to southern California. It was a good spring, but I had to apply for jobs again. There was that uncertainty I loved and hated. I loved that I didn't know where I would end up, but I also hated the fear in the back of my mind that I would end up unemployed and desperate.

After searching the job boards for a while, I finally got a reply. It wasn't from a non-profit group or government agency. It wasn't even from a university or a grad student. This was from a private, for-profit, environmental consulting firm. The work they advertised involved doing surveys for tortoises and construction monitoring in California. I had never heard of construction monitoring. I had no idea what that term meant, but they were offering more money than I had ever thought I would make in this career. I later found out that the money they are offering is actually the normal amount that a college graduate makes in most other career fields, but at that point in my life it seemed like a crazy amount of money to me.

After a few weeks doing some volunteer work—maybe to ease my conscience—I was headed to central California to work on the site of a future wind farm. This turned out to be a turning point in my life. Looking back, I often wonder where my career would have gone had I never found this job.

8 Tortoises and Hard Hats

The first few weeks of my employment as an environmental consultant were a stream of shock and confusion. After I had already quit my volunteer position, I started my new job by being told they were not going to need me. I then drove hundreds of miles back home to Phoenix, but the next morning I got a call informing me that I was going to be needed, and asking if I could make a business dinner that night. They actually paid for me to fly to California, rent a car, and book a hotel room for just one week of work during a holiday.

I later found out I was there mostly to fill in during other people's vacations. They did not think they would need me after that, so after the holiday, I was to fly back home and start looking for jobs again. So, without any other options, I grudgingly accepted what I thought would be a short-term position. I was dangerously low on funds, so I could use the thousand dollars I was going to earn in just one week of work.

I began packing as soon as I hung up the phone. I was on a

plane three hours later, and a hotel a few hours after that. I went to dinner that night and met the man who hired me. He informed me that work—again—had been delayed. I was to stay at the hotel and bill eight hours to the company for my time. The same thing happened the next day: work cancelled, bill eight hours, stay at the hotel.

By this time, my supervisor had left for his vacation. He was planning on training me the first day in the field, but since work was cancelled, he simply said, "Make sure they don't hit any tortoises," and told me that an experienced person would help me. I was lost.

The next morning, I received a phone call saying that there would be work that day. I began getting ready in my room. Things already seemed odd. Instead of my wide-brimmed field hat, I was wearing a shiny white hard hat and a bright-orange safety vest. I was wearing steel-toed boots instead of my broken-in, comfortable hiking boots. Shorts were not allowed, but that didn't bother me, since I never wore shorts in the field, anyway. The rest of my gear was mostly the same: water, sunscreen, camera, and a multi-tool, among other things. I was ready to go.

I soon pulled into a crowded parking lot of a cement factory. Everyone was wearing hard hats and vests. "Here it goes," I thought. I met with my coworker who was to help me out. I found out she was more of a surveyor, and not so much a construction monitor. We both approached the construction crews, not really knowing what would happen next.

We went through safety training, and then I drove to meet the equipment staged at an intersection of two dirt roads surrounded by miles of creosote and Joshua trees. Joshua trees are basically tall, tree-like yuccas, and are unique to the Mohave Desert. They are long-lived, and some have been around since the first white settlers arrived in the West. We were going to clear a whole field of them in order to make room for wind turbines and access roads.

I was quickly bombarded with questions from the construction crews.

"Can we cut here?"

"Can we grade there?"

"Where can we park?"

I had no answers. I thought I was just supposed to show up and tell them whether any tortoises were here or not. I was asked about equipment leaks and air quality. I was separated from my coworker quickly after the safety meeting. They were working in two areas and needed her somewhere else.

Then, the grubbing began. They simply headed off-road running a grubber (imagine a small bulldozer with a rotating wheel of metal teeth) that didn't necessarily cut the ancient trees, but grinded them to shreds; an ignoble death for the iconic trees of the Mohave Desert. They were quick workers; within a few hours they had a huge swath cut in the desert. The cut path could easily be seen from the nearby mountains.

Until now, I had spent most of my time preserving and restoring habitats. This didn't seem right. This wasn't the work of a wildlife biologist. Sure, I helped save a few snakes and squirrels from the machines, and if there were any tortoises in the area I would have saved them, as well. But it still felt dirty; in a way, I felt like I was overseeing the deaths of the animals and plants I cared so much about. I soon stopped describing my position as "wildlife biologist." It was at that point that I had officially begun my life as an "environmental consultant."

***

The second day began with more grubbing and grading. The crews were new to the desert, most coming from out of state. A common misconception is that states allow public lands to be developed to create jobs for local residents. The jobs usually go to out of state contractors who bring in their own operators from states such as New York, Texas, or Minnesota. Those operators were almost as ill-prepared as I was. They were not used to the dry desert soil, and began grading with just a single water truck to keep the dust down. The speed limit was 15 miles per hour on all dirt roads—a standard precaution for most desert work to keep the dust down and prevent wildlife casualties—so it took over an hour for the water truck to refill at the water tanks and return to the site.

Within a few minutes, there was a cloud of dust. A few minutes later, a dust wall rivaling that of the best dust storms I've seen in Phoenix. The water truck could not keep up, but they kept working anyway. California has some of the strictest air quality laws in the country, but I was new and had no idea at the time. I was just looking for threatened wildlife species to protect. They should have been shut down an hour after they started, but I wasn't sure if I had the authority to stop work.

The motor graders moved behind the grubbers, but they were too slow and the large bulldozers were soon sent in. With the dozers, they simply uprooted the brush and pushed it to the side. The dust continued to grow worse, somehow. I couldn't see more than a few feet ahead of me, and could feel dirt in my mouth and my eyes. Most of us probably got valley fever spores that day. Soon, I simply stood to the side and waited. Near the end of the day, I finally stopped work. I could not see at all, and was worried about getting hit by the flurry of equipment moving all around me. When the day was finally over, I was exhausted. I had spent ten hours in the summer heat of the Mohave, walking in front of equipment. I knew my next destination: with my blurry red eyes guiding my way I headed straight to the K-Mart for supplies.

I walked into the superstore and headed straight to the restroom, where I washed my hands and splashed water on my face. There were no paper towels. No mirrors, either. I elected to wipe my wet hands on my pants, and then swept the excess water off my face with my hand. I then exited the restroom, and headed off in search of supplies.

I was dehydrated and sun-fried. I walked to the first counter I saw. "I need goggles and a mask," I said to a young female clerk. She looked like she was in high school—petite frame, heavily made-up to look older. She looked bored, staring at a magazine. Her eyes went up and then went wide. Clearly startled, she stepped back, then composed herself. "I think we have goggles in the swim section, near the toys," she said with an extremely fake smile. She still hadn't blinked. "What about masks, I could use a painters mask," I said. She thought for a moment, and said she didn't know if they had them.

I headed toward the toy section. As I walked past the aisles, I couldn't help but get the feeling I was being looked at by other patrons. I knew I was wearing my traditional torn-up field clothing, and my hair was probably a mess from the wind and hard hat, but still, it couldn't be that bad.

I got my goggles and went to the gardening section, where I found a mask. After a few more odd looks, I paid and returned to the Holiday Inn, my new temporary home. I walked in and passed by the full-length mirror that's standard in most rooms. I froze, and took a step back. There, in the mirror, was a mad man staring at me. I was looking at a man with torn-up blue jeans that were now mostly brown. My black shirt held a circle pattern of salt stains from sweat soaking in and then drying repeatedly. My short hair seemed to form points, and stuck out jaggedly from random directions. None of this seemed too out of place from my normal field dress, but then I saw my face. My eyes were horribly blood shot, with the red veins making up most of the color, and my face was covered in what looked like war paint running down vertically over my forehead to my neck. This was how I looked when I asked for goggles and a mask with no explanation. The cashier's frightened expression now made sense to me.

After a moment of staring, I realized what happened. I had been in the dirt all day, and applied sunscreen multiple times to my face, only to get it caked with dirt again. I did this over and over for ten hours. When I splashed water on my face in the bathroom and wiped it with my hand, I had created war-like streaks of dirt on my face. Combined with everything else, I am surprised I wasn't arrested. I looked like someone that had just come back from a war in the Mohave Desert—an analogy that felt pretty accurate at the time.

The next day, I survived another round of dirt. It wasn't as bad, and I was prepared. I wore dark-tinted swimming goggles and a painter's mask the rest of the week. My outfit definitely got some snarky comments, but it was well worth it. Whenever I wasn't in the dirt cloud, I simply hooked my goggles on top of my hard hat.

The longer the project went on, the better the crews became, and the more I learned about my role as a monitor. They eventually brought more water trucks, and I was more confident with bringing up compliance issues. There wasn't another dust day like the first one, but it remained a challenge.

***

Tortoises.

That's all I heard about for months. Speed limit is 15 miles per hour for tortoises. No standing water, because it attracts ravens that kill tortoises. Look under all trucks and equipment prior to moving them to avoid running over tortoises. And of course, install miles of fencing to keep tortoises from entering the work area. They really went to extremes to protect individual tortoises, while at the same time, taking away huge swaths of habitat that would have provided food, water, and potential burrows for them. I love tortoises, but after giving environmental trainings, explaining rules about tortoises, and the constant debates about why we have to protect them, I was sick of even hearing the word "tortoise."

Several times, I was confronted about the California environmental rules. Most people seemed to think I had some control over what rules were established. I was just there to make sure they were being followed; I didn't make any of the rules. During my time there, I was insulted, screamed at, threatened, dusted by equipment, and on a few occasions, purposefully sprayed by angry water truck drivers. Even though it was definitely the minority who did those things, it left me a little bitter about consulting and working with contractors.

***

The first few months of the job, I spent my time walking in front of the grubber. It was over 100 degrees most days, and seemed to always be sunny—the Mohave Desert got a lot less summer rain than its Sonoran cousin to the south. The grubbers grinded the creosote and Joshua trees, often spitting sharp debris at my back. The workers would run right up on me when they felt I was walking too slowly, and it went that way for several miles a day. The only breaks I got were when the grubbers needed fuel, or their air filters needed changing. I'm pretty sure it was an OSHA nightmare, but I was making money. We worked six days a week, 10 to 12 hours a day. The overtime was piling up, but so was the fatigue and frustration.

By this time, my friend Colt had joined me on the project. They needed as many tortoise biologists as they could get, even though we still had yet to see a tortoise. We later met two other biologists around our age named Dirk and Bill Roy. We shared similar experiences, and eventually came to find humor in our collective situation. We all were getting worn out by the monotonous walking and the constant heat and destruction around us. More and more often, we would find ourselves going out for dinner and drinks after work. We all lived at the Holiday Inn, and usually went to a different restaurant every night.

We were given a daily stipend of money for food and a hotel. For eight months, I lived at the Holiday Inn. I am still shocked at how long I was there. I had stayed in all manner of field housing, but never saw myself living in a hotel. I got to know the staff by name and quickly racked up enough hotel points to become an elite rewards member.

While staying at a hotel can be better than sweating it out in a tent, it wasn't ideal for long-term living. It had no kitchen, so I was eating out more than I ever had in my life—at least now I could afford to eat something better than fast food—and I was again falling into bad habits of drinking too much and not getting the rest I needed. I knew this wasn't good for me, but couldn't help it. The work was stressful and exhausting, so it always felt good to kick back with friends and blow off steam after a long day.

***

During a lunch "meeting" while the boss was away and construction was slow, Dirk, Colt, and I went to town and ate at a small café near the local airport. Pictures of Burt Rutan—test pilot, experimental aircraft designer, owner of several aviation records, and local hero—were plastered all over the café. His face was even on the hot sauce. You've obviously made it big when you end up on a bottle of hot sauce.

We ate there several more times throughout the job, pretty much whenever we could sneak away. We always joked about Burt and his hot sauce. We would ask people new to the area if they knew him, and feign shock when they said they didn't. One day, while enjoying a breakfast burrito, Colt looked up. His face broke into a big grin. "It's him!" he whispered. "Who?" we both replied, and looked over our shoulders. At first, I had no recognition of the man with a few people around his table. Then I saw Colt holding the hot sauce— it was him! The hot sauce man himself, Burt Rutan. We sat there watching him, each of us telling the other to get his autograph, but all being too scared to do it. Eventually, he got up from his table and walked out of the restaurant—and our lives. We never saw Burt again. Sometimes, as a traveling wildlife biologist, it's the little stories outside of work that make the job more memorable than any other. I never would have tried all the small cafes in a couple dozen small towns with any other job, and I certainly would not have seen Burt Rutan in person, either.

During my time working consulting projects, I have stayed in many places. Tehachapi was, by far, my favorite town to stay in, and my least-favorite project to work on. The town had a weekly farmers market, the restaurants were great, and the Holiday Inn was impressive for the price. They had a yearly festival with a rodeo known as "Mountain Fest," during which the small town of 10,000 doubled in size for a rowdy country weekend.

It was always nice to see all the small town festivals while working as a traveling biologist. However, not all the places I visited were as nice. Blythe is a city in California by the Colorado River, mostly populated by the homeless, the drug-addicted, or the guards working at the local prison. It had a few fast food places, and some restaurants that were average at best. However, there was one very good barbeque joint, Rebel BBQ. It was even featured on *Tosh.0*. I lived at the Quality Inn in Blythe for six months, and ate at that place probably every other day. Other towns I have stayed in during my consulting years include the less-than-wonderful outposts of Barstow (CA), Needles (CA), Palmdale (CA), and Mesquite, (NV), but also fun and glamorous cities such as Palm Springs and Las Vegas.

***

There were two types of projects I worked on while working as a consulting biologist: renewable energy projects and transmission line projects. Both were usually associated with "green energy" production, and both were usually built on public land.

For-profit utility companies would place solar fields or wind turbines (the "green" portion) and all the associated transmission lines, substations, and access roads on public lands that were home to state and/or federally-threatened and endangered species. While I knew we needed energy and the infrastructure that goes with it, it still saddened me. It seemed cost was more important for placement of these projects than environmental impact. It was for that reason that I did not feel bad enforcing the sometimes extreme mitigation measures with construction crews. I did not feel bad when they had to make a six point turn to get to the construction site and avoid running over any undisturbed public land. It was, after all, somewhat my land. I often found myself arguing with them about preserving our public lands. Many seemed to favor giving for-profit, billion-dollar companies access and permission to destroy their hunting and recreation lands for practically free. I did not.

Transmission lines ended up being my favorite projects, by far. There wasn't as much impact, and I knew that they were needed, so I could better justify the work. I also knew placement of these lines were not nearly as flexible as energy projects are.

When I started my first transmission line project, I was shocked at how different it was from my first adventure in consulting. One day, I suddenly realized how bad the first project really was on safety. We were working in the desert again, and I remember trying to monitor the grading of an area when I was immediately stopped. We were a subcontractor, and I was stopped by the primary contractor. I was told I was way too close, and for safety, to be at least twice my current distance from the equipment—I was already twice the distance from where I was normally when in front of the grubbers on my previous project. At times, it was so strict that we weren't even allowed to be on-site while the contractors worked; we were only allowed to survey the site before construction began.

The project also required me to take mandatory breaks in my vehicle to cool off in the AC. This was actually forbidden at my other job, probably against all OSHA and desert survival recommendations. We were also required to have ice and an ice chest, an umbrella, and to check in and out with our field lead every day. I remember hearing a friend describe the needed equipment for our job to another biologist. We were used to hearing things like shovel, boots, and snake hook. Instead, it went like this: "Well, you need an umbrella…an ice chest…something to sit on…" The biologist eventually interrupted. "Wait…are we going to work or the beach?"

***

I was able to escape the desert, occasionally. For a while, I was sent to the Angeles National Forest to monitor and protect a threatened frog species on a transmission line project. I was in the mountains, among the pines and junipers. The terrain was rough, but I found another benefit of consulting: I was taken to my site by helicopter. At certain sites, they did not build roads or trails; everything was flown in. How many people can say they took a helicopter to work?

On one of my first flights, I experienced turbulence. It was a small helicopter that shifted in the wind. On the ride back, the helicopter was swaying a lot. The doors were off, and the wind was pressing against my face. The helicopter lurched, and I knew something was wrong. I gripped the hand hold and looked out the door, picking my place to jump if I had to. I then looked at the pilot to see how bad it was. He was playing with his iPhone, calm as could be. After realizing that was normal and nothing to worry about, I eventually enjoyed my time riding in the helicopter.

***

The money I made from consulting opened up opportunities I had previously thought out of reach. Because of my debt from college, and making next to nothing working for government and non-profit groups, I felt I would never be able to afford to travel out of the country. I desperately wanted to go to Australia, and after a few years of consulting, I finally did just that.

I traveled with my friend, Dirk, for a month. I would have loved to go longer, but I was on a budget, and could only take so much time off work.

Sydney was fun. We went to the famous Bondi Beach, and unexpectedly saw Prince Charles shaking hands with a large crowd of locals—what were the odds? We saw the Sydney Opera House, and got to view amazing wildlife at a local zoo. We stayed at a really fun hostel and met some great people there, even if most were much younger than us.

From Sydney, we flew to Cairns, and got there in time to view the solar eclipse. Around the city, there were signs next to all rivers and lakes warning people about crocodiles. Of course, I had to get a picture next to a sign by the water. We also got to swim with turtles and rays while snorkeling on the Great Barrier Reef.

In the city, we saw plenty of flying foxes, the largest bat species in the world. They roosted in trees right in the middle of town, would fly out by the thousands at sunset to forage during the night, and then come back at sunrise. Little baby bats clung to their mothers while hanging in trees during the day. It was quite a spectacle to see.

We drove from Cairns to Brisbane, stopping at several parks to go herping. Unfortunately, the only venomous snake we saw was a road-killed coastal taipan. We also saw some pythons and a dozen species of frogs. Despite spending hours looking at "Fang Rock" we never found any of the death adders that supposedly hang out there. One of the funnier finds was a small brown snake—or at least we thought it was a snake, at first. Since some of the non-descript brown snakes in Australia are actually some of the deadliest in the world, we didn't know how to react. We wanted to photograph the snake, but didn't want to die. The snake was also in the road and needed to be moved. After yelling back and forth whether it was safe to grab or not, we finally calmed down. We looked closer. It wasn't a snake at all, but a legless lizard. We took our pictures and moved it off the road.

The snake incident wasn't the only time the Australian wildlife made me look like a fool. I was hiking near a lake when I saw a large green lizard, larger than anything I had seen in the United States. It was very pretty and posing on a log. I wanted a picture, but it was poised above the water. I laid on my belly and crawled towards the lizard with camera in hand. I got one shot off before it got spooked and dove off the log and into the water. I was glad I got at least one. Once we arrived at Brisbane, we took a walking tour of the city and ended at the city park. There, littered about the grass and fountains like pigeons, were dozens of the same lizard. They were water dragons, and apparently very common in the cities. Nonetheless, they were still amazing, and I photographed them for quite a while.

I was sad to leave Australia, but I knew I had to. Soon, I was on a 24-hour plane ride back to the States. After taking just a few hours to recover from jet lag, I went back to watching bulldozers push dirt.

***

Before long, I started to find a balance with consulting. While the job wasn't nearly as fun as my past positions, and still required a lot of traveling, it was also enabling me to do things I never thought possible. I traveled to Australia, took a coastal tour of California, and spent time exploring the redwoods. I visited friends working with sea turtles in Texas, spent a New Year's Eve partying on the beach in San Diego, and took a week-long camping trip to parts of Arizona I had never been to. Money wasn't as tight, and I no longer had to budget everything. I was able to help my struggling family members, donate to environmental groups, and buy decent field gear. It was definitely a tradeoff for not loving the work I was doing on a daily basis.

During one of the more frustrating times of consulting, I released a manifesto of sorts. While it was done mainly as a joke to relieve stress, I feel it pretty accurately describes the nature of the work, and how frustrating and mind-numbing it can be. The following list quickly became popular with my coworkers:

Scott's official rules of consulting
1. Never volunteer for anything (unless it's to go home early).
2. Never take the initiative (unless the end result will be going home early).
3. Always do what's easy. No exceptions.
4. Complain.
5. Avoid leaving your vehicle. Better a hundred tortoises die than you getting out to move them.
6. Threaten to quit no less than once a month.
7. F.R.E.D. reports (our daily monitoring reports) are optional on Fridays.
8. Always ask to be on a different crew, and after you're switched, complain more.
9. The roads to the gas station with ice cream also need to be monitored.
10. Always blame the man.

9 Desert Life (Part Three)

After about a year of working long days for six days a week and dealing with construction, I was ready for a break. I wanted to remember why I became a biologist, and staring at excavators and bulldozers wasn't it. I left my company, and really wasn't sure I would ever be back. I had applied—and was immediately accepted—for my old seasonal position surveying for tortoises in Nevada and California.

I know it seems silly to leave a secure, high-paying job to go back to making little money with no job security, but that's what I did. I left the hotel and restaurant life for the tent and camp stove. And I was happy—for a while, anyway.

Colt had also decided to leave consulting a few months earlier. He had gone back to work with sea turtles, and now that their nesting season had ended, he was coming back to work with tortoises again, as well. But aside from Colt being there again, the rest of the crew had changed considerably from the previous year. Most of them had little experience with the desert and camping. One member had never pooped outside of his own home; it was going to be a learning experience for him. There were a few girls on the crew this year, and all had done previous field work. When it was time to choose a field partner, everyone paired up, ignoring Colt and myself. Later, I found out it was because everyone was under the impression we had already decided to be partners. I wasn't upset in the least how things turned out; it would be just like old times.

***

Like the year before, we began our training for the upcoming field season with the StyroTort training lines. This portion of the training basically consisted of walking designated lines through the desert, and trying to find Styrofoam tortoises hidden along the way.

I felt a little silly looking for "styrotorts" in the desert for the second year in a row, but I got through it. The previous year, Colt and I did very well, but this year we had rushed, and our detection curve suffered. We just wanted to get to the camping, and more importantly, finding tortoises (real tortoises, not Styrofoam ones). We both had a passion for finding wildlife—snakes, birds, mammals, whatever—we just wanted to see things we wouldn't see in the cities. It was almost a competition for us and the other crewmembers. Who could find more tortoises? It was good to be back.

***

Our housing had greatly improved from the previous year. We now had two houses, so there were only two people per room. Seeing how we spent so much time with our field partners, we elected to bunk with other people.

The field season took place during the height of the housing crisis in Las Vegas. We were getting a nice upscale house for way less than it would have been the year before. I have stayed in just about every type of field housing possible, and this was the best, so far— huge kitchen, three bathrooms, and five bedrooms. The best part was the swimming pool-sized hot tub in the back yard. In fact, we didn't know it was a hot tub until we found the controls. Having a hot tub at home certainly made for a lot of interesting nights and fun memories.

Being with a younger crew really taught me the meaning of the joke that goes something like this: "I think of myself as being in my twenties...until I hang out with twenty year olds. Then, I think,

'No, I'm thirty.'" They would play beer pong and poker until early in the morning, and then be up a few hours later with no problem. These obviously weren't things I could do regularly anymore and survive.

We lived near the Red Rock Casino, and that became our favorite weekend hangout spot. Tired from all the hiking and camping during the week, we didn't feel like taking a bus or cab to the strip, so we usually opted for the Red Rock. They had bowling, bars, and darts. Many nights, we wouldn't head home until after 2 AM.

We lived in a gated community, but never found the gate key, so most nights started and ended with us jumping over the fence to get in and out. I really felt like a teenager again, running through the streets with my friends, jumping fences, and getting into trouble. I wonder what the neighbors thought of the group of rowdy twenty-somethings (and almost thirty-somethings, in my case) running through the streets at the wee hours of the night. It was a fun spring, both in the field, and at home.

***

That season, the weather changed yet again. Instead of facing heat or snow, it was wind. For weeks at a time, it would blow in our faces, and seemed to change direction as we turned each corner of our survey plots.

The wind provided many challenges. Besides pelting us with sand and dirt, it would make it hard to communicate. If the person walking in the back fell behind or stopped, it was hard to hear his yell through the wind, so we had to look back every so often. There were several times where we got separated in the rolling hills and bajadas (sediment deposits that result from water running down mountains).

The most challenging part of working in the wind was setting up tents. I rarely used my tent, but once, during training, there was no room for me to lay in the bed of the truck, so I set it up. The wind was fierce that night, and we all were having trouble with our tents, except one person. He sat there talking about how easy his flip-out tent was and how we should have bought one of those. Over and over he bragged, then, finally took out his tent. He flipped it out and it took full form instantly, just has he said. Then, with little warning the wind gusted, his tent bowed out, and with a poof sound it slipped his hand and took flight. The tent rose like a kite and flew hundreds of feet in the air to the west. We all watched in awe. All of us wanted to laugh after the bragging, but we held it in. After the tent owner ran off in the distance, chasing his tent, all of us completely lost it.

In the end, despite dealing with all the wind, I was glad to be back sleeping under the stars.

***

After being in the desert season after season, you begin to think you've seen everything. It's always fun and exciting to see wildlife, but you lose at least a little of the amazement you felt the first time. I thought I had seen and done it all until the last week of the season.

I was hiking at the translocation site. It had been a busy day, and I had seen several snakes and a few tortoises. It was getting hot out, and I was looking forward to getting done with my line. I saw a huge burrow—way too big for a tortoise—and knew it was a mammal burrow. I wandered over, thinking I would just see some scat or tracks. I shined my light in the hole and was shocked. There, huddled together, were at least eight coyote pups at the back of the burrow. They squinted and looked at me, barely able to lift their heads. It must have been a fresh litter. They were adorable—and I rarely describe things as adorable.

I then started wondering where mama was. I looked around, and quickly spotted a coyote in the distance. I stood and watched. She wasn't coming closer, but was keeping an eye on things, walking large circles around me. Time to go. I left the area knowing that she would most likely move the pups to a new burrow after my intrusion.

Later that same week, I had another encounter with a coyote. I had just left a kit fox burrow where I had observed several kit foxes sticking their heads out of a hole, only to go inside and having another head come out of a different hole. It reminded me of a "whack-a-mole" game. I was walking near a wash when I heard a pathetic yip. I turned and saw a slightly older coyote pup prancing around. I think it was lost. It would jog a few steps and let out its pathetic yip, wait, then proceed in a different direction. It clearly was not paying attention when it jogged within a few yards of me and did the yip again. It was so cute in its own pathetic way. It looked up, and was shocked to see I wasn't its mother. It quickly ran the other way into the distance.

This time, I did not see mama. I sadly started thinking of the possibilities of what happened. Mother killed, or another male coyote finding the weak young. I stopped thinking. It was too cute to start thinking like that.

***

My time in Las Vegas had come and gone quickly. In the last few weeks, I had watched all my coworkers search for jobs and interview for positions. They were going to grad school or doing bird surveys on the coast. I heard some talk about work in Wyoming and Idaho, and I soon began to think about where I was going. I decided I wasn't ready to stare at construction equipment quite yet. Sure, consulting work needed good biologists that weren't afraid to shut down projects and halt construction to save animals. But it wasn't going to be me. Not yet.

I began to apply for work. Within a few hours, I found the position I wanted. For the next few months, I was going to be in southern Georgia working on an ecological research station, assisting the herpetology department. I felt the excitement that had been missing for a while. I would be going to an area I had never been before, finding animals I had never seen. In addition, while I didn't know it at the time, I was also on my way to meet up with old friends.

10 Old Friends and Alligators

Before heading to Georgia, I enjoyed two weeks at home. Most jobs never quite line up back to back, so a traveling field biologist usually enjoys a few weeks between seasons to go home or to get to the new job.

The two weeks flew by, and I was soon packing again. I was going to be driving my beat-up old truck across the country. From Phoenix, Arizona, to southern Georgia. It was a few hours longer than my trip several years ago to Missouri, and this time, I was driving solo.

I started the trip with no problems. I drove I-10 south and then east. I resisted stopping to see "The Thing" at a roadside stand near Tucson. It had always been a dream of mine to travel with someone and stop by all the roadside attractions from coast to coast. My ex and I were too busy when we drove to Missouri from Arizona a few years ago, and I didn't feel up to it on my own. That changed on the first day as I was looking for somewhere to stop.

I was in Texas now, and needed to rest. I had made good time, so I pulled out my map. At this time, I still refused to pay for a smartphone, and didn't trust the dashboard GPS systems. No, I was one of the few remaining map and compass guys. I settled on Fort Stockton after seeing an advertisement for "The World Largest Road Runner Statue."

Nearing the town, I crossed a Border Patrol check point. I groaned. My truck was packed solid with gear, clothing, and supplies. The officer walked up and looked in. After looking at my beat-up Ford Ranger, he asked if he could look inside. I knew all the backpacks and duffel bags probably looked suspicious. Reluctantly, I agreed. He opened the passenger door and looked around. He settled on my ice chest, flipped it open, and saw my boxes of cliff bars and Gatorade. He looked up and directed me to move on. All that and he only looked at my ice chest? As I was driving away I began to think maybe he was just hungry and hoped I had a sandwich to confiscate. Then, I started thinking about sandwiches. It was time to stop soon.

Fort Stockton seemed like the typical desert town—strip malls mixed with older buildings, and lots of hotels and gas stations to support the interstate traffic. I found my hotel and passed out quickly. I had a big day tomorrow. I was going to drive to Louisiana and stop at the town of Hammond, where the first season of *In the Heat of the Night* was filmed. I also was going to see the largest road runner statue in the world tomorrow. Big day.

I found my way to the statue early the next day. It was as big as a monster truck and very detailed. After taking a photo and standing there quietly to get full appreciation of what was in front of me, I realized I was done with the statue. It was not something that required a pause for reflection; it was just a big road runner. So, I jumped back in my truck and was off to Hammond, and then Georgia.

If you have not driven Interstate 10 from Texas to Georgia, I would suggest it. There are mile-long bridges over swamps. I was driving through the year they had major flooding—I always seemed to be traveling during extreme weather events—so it was even more interesting seeing the miles of submerged swamp all around me. I imagined having to hike to the nearest town through the swamp. It was a scary thought.

***

I soon arrived at the small research station in rural Georgia. It was located near a town of about 5000 thousand people. The town had a bar, a dollar store, and a grocery store. It wasn't much, but that was all I needed.

My housing was a small, two-bedroom cabin. I had two younger roommates that were sharing a room. Finally, my experience and age got me some manner of respect: my own room. The cabin was well-furnished and very comfortable. From the porch, we had a great view of trees covered in Spanish moss, and an open field beyond.

I was walking distance to the research center and to a small, historic general store. I'm sure the only customers were employees of the research center. The research center was larger than I had imagined. In fact, it was bigger than any place I had worked before, much larger than the Arizona Game and Fish office. It had a computer lab, library, and individual lab rooms for all the different research groups. There was a lab for habitat, fisheries, herps, and tortoises, a shared lab for all the grad students, and offices for the heads of the research groups. There was also a maintenance compound and a shop. In addition to being a research station, the complex also served as ranch. It was funded by the former owner of Coca-Cola. While research was its main focus, it often hosted hunting events for donors.

Overall, the place was well taken care off. Controlled burns kept the invasive species out, the ticks and chiggers down, and allowed the native flora to flourish. I was excited to start.

***

I was to help with all manner of research projects, the main one having to do with predator exclusion. I checked snake traps and pitfall traps every other day. There was only one issue: part of the exclusion included an electric fence that surrounded all the trapping areas.

The first day, I went out with my new field partner. She was KJ's (from Missouri) girlfriend. Small world, I thought. KJ had worked here after we had all left MOFEP, and had met her while working here. She was athletic, having played sports in college. When we came to the fence, she was quickly able to put a five gallon bucket down and jump the fence with ease. I watched, and then it was my turn. I do not recall anyone ever calling me an agile person. My work in the desert was more of a trudging march than a graceful hike. I was even called "the moose" for a while in Missouri. I wasn't afraid of getting shocked, but where I would be getting shocked. I was going to be straddling an electric fence five to ten times a day, every other day.

The first day, I made it over the fence. The line had grazed against my jeans, but did not shock me. We checked our traps and exited the enclosure. We jumped the fence six times that day to check all of our traps. At several points we could use the truck to help out. Only six times and I already had a close call. Three months of this did not bode well; I was bound to slip up at least once.

The second week, I was on my own. When I made a joke about straddling the fence and slipping, I was informed that if I was worried I could always flip the breakers before I go in. It had already been a full week, and I was just now being informed about this. I decided to flip the breakers until I got used to jumping the fences.

I later arrived at an enclosure, and after a little searching, found the first breaker. It looked like no one had used it in months; it stood alone next to the road and the fence, tall grass growing around it. I parked the truck and approached it. I was in a hurry, so I flipped the lid and started to reach in. Buzzzzz! I caught movement and jumped back. Erupting from the breaker box was a steady stream of red flying things. What else could they be? Wasps. Of course it would be wasps. When I jumped back, I dropped the lid, which was a heavy wooden slab. It swung on its hinges and banged against the side of the box, causing an even bigger eruption of wasps.

I controlled myself enough to only run a few hundred feet away, and considered my options. Electric shock or facing an angry swarm of wasps. I chose the fence. I ran by the breaker box quickly, closed the lid, and continued toward the traps.

Through all my time working at the station, I only shocked myself twice. The first time I touched the fence with my hand, just to see how bad it was. I am not going to lie—it hurt. The second time was just how I had imagined: I was halfway over when the bucket moved and I lost my balance. Luckily, the fence only caught my inner thigh, but it still woke me up and made me more cautious.

***

My old friend, KJ, arrived for a visit to see his girlfriend shortly after I had started work. Of course, while he was here we had to go herping. The best part of being away from the desert was all the water everywhere. We had a creek in my back yard, so we decided to go snorkeling to look for turtles. Later in the season, I would actually get paid to do this, but this time was just for fun. We would still record any interesting or relevant data we found for the research station, but we really just wanted to see what we could find. I suited up in my snorkel gear and met KJ and a few others in the water.

We formed a loose survey line, which quickly dissolved into people meandering wherever they thought looked good. I remember swimming in the center, and someone saying something about the deep spots. "What about them?" I asked, having just dove to the bottom of one. "That's where a lot of turtles hang out, but also where you're gonna find the gators this time of year." Suddenly, I felt like an idiot.

Alligators! Of course there were going to be alligators. This was southern Georgia, but for whatever reason, I had just never really considered the possibility of running into alligators. I was swimming in a creek that definitely contained alligators, and had just dove into the murky deep water where they are known to hide out. I felt a slight bit of panic. I never really felt afraid when hiking, I guess because I knew I could take action. Run, fight, hide, I could do something. In the water, I was definitely out of my element; there was no running or hiding from the alligators. If they chose to attack—which was extremely rare—there wasn't much I could do. I looked around, but no one seemed concerned. I decided I wasn't going to miss out on finding turtle species I had never seen because of alligators. I took a deep breath and got back to looking, even if I did avoid some of the murkier, deeper water.

***

Throughout the season, I went snorkeling for turtles several more times. The research center marked certain species of turtles, and was always ready to get more samples. One of the last times I went snorkeling, I was reminded of how dedicated herpers really are.

I met my field partner and another lab member at the river. We had all brought the usual gear, snorkels, and masks, as well as tubs to put any turtles we found. It was a hot day, and I was excited to get in the water, alligators and all. I had only seen one, so far, and it had been far up the river in a deep, wider spot.

We began swimming around, looking under logs and near large rocks in the water—normal spots for turtles to hang out while underwater. We checked those places, as well as the deeper spots of the river. I went down to check under a larger rock in the water. When I came up, I heard something splashing. I looked around and saw my field partner was next to a log with her head barely above water, struggling to stay afloat. My first though was that she must be caught on the log and that the current had her pinned. I threw my snorkel gear off and swam over. When I got to her I yelled, "Where are you caught?" not wanting to make things worse by blindly pulling on her. She started to talk, but was pulled down, then popped back up. She managed to say, "Turtle," and suddenly, everything became clear.

She had found an alligator snapping turtle, and refused to let go of her prize. It had wedged itself under the log. We both took hold, and with a coordinated effort, removed the prehistoric turtle from its hiding spot. It was the first one I had seen in the wild, and it really did look like a dinosaur. It had a spiked back and spikes on the side of its shell. It was covered in moss and held its beak open, ready to snap at anything that got too close. I could see its worm like tongue (used to lure fish) wriggling in its mouth. It was an intimidating species, to say the least.

We quickly got it in the tub. After all the excitement, we decided to call it a day and take the turtle back to the lab for processing. We would then release it later, and of course, take some photographs.

I had nothing but the greatest respect for my field partner, and time and time again, she reminded me why.

***

I started working in Georgia at an awkward time. In other areas, rain had been prevalent, but in southern Georgia there was a persistent drought. Of course, this meant all the wildlife had to do its best to adjust. The alligators mostly went to the larger rivers or the deep holes in the swamps and creeks. The frogs were less common, and there were no salamanders around. The reptiles seemed to be doing okay, but like the gators, the turtles were all making their way to the larger river. I was told the mosquitoes were not nearly as bad as usual, but the gnats were worse than ever. The thing about gnats is that they don't seem to care about bug spray. Maybe it was because I was using a non-DEET spray and only spraying my hat, but either way, it was not working. I would end up with gnats in my mouth, up my nose, and in my eyes. When holding equipment, or even snakes, I could not shoo them away from my face. No, I would just have to endure it.

I spent some of my time tracking rat snake movements. Transmitters were installed in the snakes, and weekly locations were recorded. We were tracking their movements and what habitat they used over the course of the year. By doing this, we could help the research station figure out what conservation measures to implement.

It was interesting playing hide-and-seek with snakes. We would track them to a small area and then try to find their hiding place. Whether in a tree, underground, or in the water, it was always amazing how well they blended in.

***

Living in a community of biologists was not what I was used to. Before, I was usually with a small group of people that all worked on the same project. This, on the other hand, was a whole community of thirty or so people that lived on-site working on all sorts of different projects.

After work, there was always a variety of activities to take part in. Some nights, we would put up a sheet and have an outdoor movie night using a projector. Sometimes we would simply put a white sheet out and shine a light on it, to see all the different species of insects it attracted. There was a gym on-site, and sometimes people volunteer to teach specialty classes.

I was always trying new things. I had fallen out of that habit while doing consulting, so I decided to try again. I was going to a yoga class taught by another old friend from the Missouri crew that was staying on-site to work on a grad school project. This would be my first time trying yoga.

I was nervous as I approached the building. I knew I wasn't flexible, and would rationalize it by quoting the movie *Zombieland*: "You ever see a lion stretch before it pounces on a gazelle?" I knew it was flawed statement, but I liked it none the less. The building was built on a raised platform, and my footsteps made loud, hollow thumps as I walked in. I took my space in the back and began.

At first, I was doing fine with the warrior pose and child's pose. Then, there were some other poses that had me leaning over. I suddenly lost my balance and crashed to the floor. The hollow floor boomed and the whole class jumped. That was my last yoga class. After that, I elected to go to the gym or look for turtles in my spare time.

***

Since coming to the South, I had noticed something: everything just seemed bigger out here. Both the snakes and lizards seemed much larger than those found in the deserts of the Southwest.

One day in late summer, I found on the road an eastern diamondback rattlesnake—one of the largest venomous snakes in the United States. It was massive. It looked similar to the western diamondback rattlesnakes of the Southwest, but the diamond pattern was more colorful, with dark greens and browns forming the pattern on its back. This snake was on the road and did not want to move. I looked at my four-foot-long snake hook and at the snake, which was about the same size. Suddenly, I wished I had a bigger hook. The snake was as wide as a soft ball bat and about as long. Despite the prevalence of manipulated photographs passed around the internet, any rattlesnake over four feet long is actually pretty rare. With this snake, the girth was just as impressive as the length (insert joke here). It was easily twice as wide as its western relative. I eventually got it on the hook, and the weight caused my hook to bow slightly.

Rattlesnakes weren't the only species that were much larger in the South. The most surprising catch for me was the coachwhip I found on my eighth week of the job. I was checking traps when I came to my last one of the day. I walked to the trap, leaned over to look inside, and chaos erupted. A brown mass flailed from one side of the cage to the other. Then, I saw what it was: a large, brown, nonvenomous snake, a coachwhip. Coachwhips are interesting creatures. Rather than waiting in ambush, they are true hunters, and have blinding speed and lightning reflexes that they use to chase and catch prey. They even have been known to catch emerging bats out of mid-air. They are also one of the most defensive snakes I have run into, often repeatedly striking when approached or captured. In this case, I had a seven-foot-long coachwhip staring at me through the wire mesh.

I looked into the snake trap. The trap itself was a drift fence similar to those I used in Missouri, but the fence led to a funnel and then into a six by six foot box made of metal mesh fencing. The box was only about three feet tall and had a wooden roof and floor. We removed the snakes from a two by two foot hatch on top of the cage. It was hard to reach some areas of the trap to catch the snakes, and coachwhips tended to find those hard-to-reach areas more often than not. The seven footer was in the one of those areas. I was going to have to lean my entire upper body in the trap to reach the snake.

I opened the cage and stuck my head in. The coachwhip was already in a defensive pose. I knew I was going to get bit before I even reached my hand in. I took a breath and reached for the waiting snake. I saw a streak of brown and felt pain in my wrist. I instinctively pulled my hand back. There was blood. Again, I reached in, and again I was struck. This time, I tried to keep reaching, and got tagged twice more. Just as I was going to get a firm hold of the snake, it darted from its hiding spot toward the other side of the cage. In doing, so it was coming straight at my face. I was half in the trap and half out. I jumped and hit my head on the roof of the cage. Then, I lost site of the snake—a disconcerting feeling when it's a seven-foot snake, even if it is nonvenomous. I quickly turned, and located the snake. My hesitation was quickly turning to frustration. I was already bleeding from my hand, but I gritted my teeth and reached again, slow and steady this time, so I wouldn't miss. It struck again, but I didn't react. It was easier once I had already been bitten a few times. I finally seized the snake, and it firmly latched on my wrist with its jaws one last time. Better than my face, I suppose.

Once I pulled the snake from the trap, I was amazed at its length. It was taller than me and very thick. I thought for sure it had to be a record. When I got it back to the lab, I equipped it with a pit tag, which is a small, electronic tag about the size of a grain of rice that is inserted into the snake using a needle, and used for tracking purposes. It is also used on many other species, including sea turtles, and is similar to the microchips put in pets. During the tagging process, I checked for the record length. I had missed it by a few inches. To think there were larger snakes out there was a crazy thought. However, it also brought me comfort knowing that wild areas, even in the U.S., still had things like that in them.

I also thought about people's fear of snakes. This was, by far, the largest snake I had seen in the wild. It had bit me several times and didn't hold back. I bled a little, but it stopped on its own before I even got to the truck. I thought about some of my other injuries over the years. I had actually been hurt more by small mammals like mice and squirrels than any nonvenomous snake bite I had received, even the multiple ones I got from that monster coachwhip.

***

Due to the drought in Georgia, I was missing out on some of the wildlife that the South was famous for. I still had not seen all of the frog species I was hoping to see. In particular, there was one species of tree frog I had yet to see, but desperately wanted to find, as my time in Georgia was coming to an end. It was the cricket tree frog that I was after.

I was nearing my last week on the job, and the rains finally arrived. I began to hear new frog calls, and see more amphibian captures in my traps. However, I still hadn't found my target tree frog, and was beginning to think I wouldn't get to see one before I left.

After a day of checking my traps, I was driving home. I had decided to take a different route back, through the maze of dirt roads on the research property. I turned the corner and saw why this road wasn't taken very often. A large tree branch full of leaves hung over the road. I stopped and measured. I would be able to make it under the tree limb, but would be driving through the leaves. It was too far for me to back up, so I went for it. I pull forward and the leaves covered my windshield, kind of like driving into a car wash. When I emerged from the other side, my windshield was covered in wet leaves and excess water from the earlier rains. I was about to hit my wipers when one of the leaves moved. I looked closer. It was a tree frog, and the one I had been hoping to see before I left. With dull green skin, it was not as pretty as some of the other species, but I was happy to see it. It felt like the station was giving me a goodbye gift.

**

During the last week of my time in Georgia, I was assisting a grad student who was researching turtle movements. This required a large sample size over a large geographic area. Because of this and other reasons, snorkeling was not going to be sufficient, so we installed turtle traps along the river.

Turtle traps work the same way as many bird traps, snake traps, and fish traps. The trap is a cylindrical, wire mesh structure with floaters on it, and a flexible funnel on each side. The idea is to place it in the water and have the turtles swim inside. Once inside, they have a hard time finding the opening out. The floaters are used so the trap stays partially above water, allowing the turtles to come up for air. The traps are baited with punctured cans of tuna. The puncture allows the scent to escape, but not the meat. We set these traps all along the river and checked them every day.

I saw several different species of turtles while assisting that week, and was always anxious to see what was in the traps. Occasionally, we would find fish or other non-target species in the traps, which we would release. This was one of my favorite times during my work in Georgia.

By this time, the rains had finally come and the water level had risen a few feet. This meant most of our traps were in deeper water now, which required us to wade in waist-deep to access them. The water had also turned a murky brown color, and you could not see more than an inch down. This really didn't bother me until I came to one, specific trap.

We had separated to make things go quicker, and my partner was several hundred meters away checking her own traps. I began to walk down the bank toward mine. I saw a large log floating next to my turtle trap. It must have gotten stuck I thought. It was an odd-shaped log, and when I came closer, the "log" suddenly shifted and then submerged with a flick of its tail. An alarm went off in my head. Logs don't have tails. I stood on the bank looking at the spot where, moments ago, a six-foot alligator had been floating. The spot was right next to my turtle trap.

I began going over my options. I could leave and tell the others I wasn't going to check the trap, or maybe I could try to reach the trap with a stick. Looking at how far out the trap was in the water, I knew this wasn't practical. Finally, I decided to brave the water and check the trap quickly.

I entered the brown muddy water slowly. At each step, I was expecting to hit a solid moving mass, but it didn't happen. I reached the trap. I tried to lift it and realized the line holding it in place was caught. I was waist-deep, and wanted out of the water. I jerked the trap several times, but the line would not give. Then, I realized the bait was still in the trap. By thrashing around, I was really just getting more of the tuna smell in the water. Like the people you see on Shark Week, I was pretty much chumming the water all around me. I knew I had to feel down the rope and find the weight. I leaned over, my face now even with the dirt brown water, and the sound track to jaws popped in my head. I found the weight with my hand and detached it from a rock it was lodged under. Then, I drug the whole trap out.

The trap was empty. I decided to replace it in the shallower water. That was the last time I assisted checking traps. Not because of alligators, but because I was moved to other projects. Not long after, my time was up at the research station. I only saw alligators twice while I was there, both times near the same area of the creek. It's funny, some of the people that swim in the waters there all the time think I'm crazy for handling rattlesnakes, and couldn't understand why I was worried about swimming with alligators. To each their own, I suppose.

***

I could have stayed in Georgia (I had been offered an extension), but by this time, I was low on funds, some of my family had not yet fully recovered from the recession, and I was going to be turning 30 years old soon. I decided that staying and making eight dollars an hour wasn't a decision I could justify anymore, and that I had to start thinking about the future. I hated leaving, and I told myself that if money wasn't an issue I would travel around doing these seasonal jobs forever. I was obviously lying to myself; I wanted a home, and eventually a family. I also knew deep down that I wanted those things in Arizona.

It was hard giving them my final notice. I was heading back to the West, and back to consulting. The job was in Nevada, but that was close enough to home, for now. I drove back quickly so I could get there by the starting date (I skipped the largest roadrunner statue this time around).

11 One Last Time

I stayed in consulting for two more years. I paid off debt, helped my family and put together a nice savings. Then, the urge hit me again. I was tired of hotels and bulldozers. I wanted to go home, for good. I wanted to go back to Arizona.

I had been monitoring the job boards for a while now, and soon found a job in Arizona. It was tortoise work for the same person I had worked with during my previous stint with Arizona Game and Fish. This time, it would be closer to home. I would get to sleep in my own bed at a house I had not seen much of for the past two years. I had to apply. Even if it was only for four months, it would be the longest I would have been home in nearly four years.

When the interview finally came, I was nervous. What must they think of me, leaving a permanent, well-paying position, to go back to seasonal work making what first-year technicians make. My boss at the consulting firm did not understand, but respected my decision. My coworkers that had similar backgrounds working for non-profits understood, while those that started consulting right after college did not. I didn't care, because I understood. This was what I wanted.

I found out later that I was offered the job after a near split-decision on whether to hire me or not. It came down to one vote. The deciding vote turned out to be my crew leader for the season—I like to think I didn't disappoint. So, I was off to Arizona. This was to be my last stint as a seasonal biologist. I was going to gain full-time employment with the department, or resign myself to a life of consulting. It was my last shot.

***

The job was similar to what I did a few years ago. It was a tortoise occupancy study on various government-owned lands. The research plots were several hundred square meters, and we hiked the entire interior of the plot on specific transects. When we found tortoises we would mark them the same as we did before and record the same data. We would also look for scat, tracks, and burrows.

We did not work in wilderness areas that year, so there were no four-mile treks to reach our plots. All of the study plots were usually within 500 meters of a dirt road. While the hiking to reach the plots was not as bad, the terrain was worse than what I remembered. These plots were located in the Sonoran Desert, and mostly in rocky, mountainous areas. Most hills had at least one side completely covered with jumping cholla.

The crew was smaller, and there was less ground to cover. Instead of traveling around most of the state, we were focusing our efforts on two study sites. One was near Buckeye (where I was living at the time), and the other, the harder of the two, was near Casa Grande.

***

The thing I liked most about the job was going home at night. I could actually cook on a daily basis, slept in my own bed for four months straight, and saw my friends and family daily.

I could start doing normal things I hadn't done since college. I could meet up with my roommate to watch a game or have dinner. I could volunteer or join a community group that met weekly. I could make plans during the work week, since I would not be camping. I could also actually start normal dating again.

Before this job, I usually only had relationships with people in similar career fields. They seemed to be the only ones that could understand and tolerate my work schedule for more than a few weeks. I was really happy to be home, and was wanting it to stay this way for more than the four months the job was scheduled for.

***

Besides enjoying being at home, I was enjoying seeing quite a bit of wildlife on our sites. I saw the usual deer, rattlesnakes, lizards, and hawks. I also saw plenty of tortoises, including a three-legged old guy that probably lost a leg to a coyote along the way. Then, I saw something I had yet to see until that last season in the field.

It was middle of the season, and I was near Casa Grande. This was the harder of the two sites, with steep, black rock mountains covered with jumping cholla. The site I was on had nearly vertical rock faces in some places. That meant climbing down, then over, and then back up, on every transect. I was near the top of one of the steeper climbs when I noticed a large cave. This area seemed to be too steep for tortoises, but the cave was very inviting. I climbed up and leaned on the mouth of the cave, as it was the only flat ground I could find. I heard movement from the back of the cave, and something shifted slightly in the darkness. I pulled out my flashlight and peered inside. I saw a tail with a rattle on it a few meters into the cave. It was attached to a large black-tailed rattlesnake. I looked at the odd snake. It seemed too long and had too many curves, and then I realized it was two snakes lying together. I lifted the light and found yet another snake, then another. This cave was filled with black-tailed rattlesnakes. I counted at least six of them all coiled together. Their age and size varied from young and smaller individuals to much older and larger snakes. The biggest was perhaps a little over four feet long.

The snakes started to stir, and I called my coworkers over. It took some convincing because of how steep the climb was, but they eventually came up. We took pictures and stared in amazement. I had never seen a rattlesnake hibernaculum before. We left before the snakes stirred too much, because if they did start our way, there wasn't much room to maneuver quickly, especially with three of us crammed in such tight, steep quarters.

***

Of all my jobs over the years, the hiking on tortoise jobs was the most strenuous and dangerous. Over the years, I had a number of close calls; trips and falls that could have been a lot worse than they were. I ended up with bruises, scratches, and cuts almost daily.

The worst injury of my career happened a month before the season would have ended. I was hiking on one of the worst plots near Buckeye. It was a steep, rocky mountain, completely covered with jumping cholla. I often would end up with cholla spines in my ankle or calf on this plot even when I didn't fall. Jumping cholla is a segmented cactus with rigid, barbed spines one to two inches long. Each segment is cylinder-shaped, and contains hundreds of spines. The end segments are often called balls. The jumping, or teddy bear, cholla spreads by the end segments attaching to any animal (or careless person) passing by that brushes against it. The weight of the ball is enough pressure for the razor sharp spines to penetrate skin, and the barbs keep the spines embedded. The animal will then carry the cholla to a new area. The end segments are so loose the wind will often be enough to detach them. This leaves many four to six inch cholla balls laying at the base of the cactus.

I was walking a plot I had surveyed once before, and thought about how dangerous it was. I started my second transect on the steepest part of the mountain. I was half way up looking for snakes, tortoises, and cholla balls. I was forced to weave around the thicker patches of cholla. I was picking my way through the steep, rocky terrain above one of those patches when I took a wrong step. A small, fist-sized rock had rolled under my foot. I tried shifting my weight to the opposite foot, but that foot was on top of a larger rock. The added weight was too much for that rock, and it too gave away. Suddenly, I was wind-milling my arms, desperately training to regain my balance. I said aloud, "No, no, no, NO, NOOOOO!" I was headed down straight into the thick cholla patch that I had hiked above trying to avoid. In a last ditch effort to keep from rolling down the whole mountain, I dropped my left leg and guided my fall on one side. I landed directly on top of a five-foot-wide cholla. I felt the barbs pierce my light weight field pants (I had given up on jeans a few weeks earlier). I used my hands to brace myself and keep my face clear. The pain was intense, but my adrenaline was up. The rocks underneath gave way, and so did the cactus. My plan did not work; I began rolling down the hill and directly over all the cholla and rocks.

I'm not sure how many rolls I did before finally skidding to a stop. Cholla had pierced my hands, and I had half a dozen cholla balls sticking out of my arms. An entire cactus had been uprooted and was stuck in my backpack and my butt. My body weight had pushed in the cholla spines as far as they could go—all the way into my muscle tissue—during my roll down the hill. Several cholla balls had pierced under my knee cap, and I could feel the spines underneath. Many had broken off under the skin or muscle during the roll. I would estimate that I had over 2000 barbed spines in me, and half a dozen rock fragments under my skin. I maintained enough sense to at least cover my neck and face during the fall, and was relatively clear in those areas. While the spines got dangerously close, my private areas were also unscathed.

I stood there frozen, afraid to move. Then, all at once I let out the most terrified, and loudest scream I have ever made. It echoed through the mountains and reached my field partner a hundred meters away on the other side of the mountain. He came running. To his credit, he arrived quickly. He stood staring at me. "What do you need?" he asked. "I don't know…help?" I really didn't know. I remembered the deer fawn I had found dead in a similar cholla patch all those years ago. I didn't know how bad it was, how deep the needles went, or if I had torn anything on the fall. I had been afraid to move. I moved my ankle, and felt a jolt of pain. The other ankle was numb for holding most of my weight for so long. I tried to move my leg. My quad muscle seized up like a rock, and I was hit by more intense pain. "I can't hike out of here," I said. That was the only thing I knew for sure.

After some discussion, my partner called 911. He then called the military officer in charge of the survey area, followed by our supervisor at AZGFD. While we waited for help, I began pulling out some of the cholla balls. The first to go was the entire uprooted cactus on my butt. I could feel the weight of the cactus pulling on my ass. I used a stick to get it off my back pack and then I shook; I was clinging to the side of a mountain, covered in cholla, and shaking my ass. The entire cactus began to peel off me. It was like peeling a band aid, but a thousand times worse. Once that was done, we were able to get my backpack off and get my multitool out.

My field partner left to get the first aid kit out of the truck and flag down the help that was coming. We were nearly half a mile from a lone, two-track road. I began pulling on the first cholla ball. The spines would not release the skin on my hand; instead, the skin stretched. Finally, when the pain seemed unbearable, one by one the spines came out with a popping sensation. I felt nauseated, but pulled out half a dozen more. My eyes watered, and I was muttering every swear word I could think of, but resisted crying out. Finally, I couldn't take anymore. The ones lodged in my muscles would not release at all. My body had begun shaking uncontrollably. I took a new approach as I was still waiting for help. I began cutting the needles and discarding the cholla balls. Once I was rid of the cholla balls I could finally sit and concentrate on the individual needles.

The first help arrived about an hour after my partner called. Somehow, our call for medical help had turned into a "lost hiker" call. I was met by mountain rescue. They informed me that a helicopter was on its way to get me out. This seemed like overkill. I began to say I could walk, but before I could finish, the rescuers screamed, "You can walk!" I quickly backtracked. "I can limp," I said. "I can't use my quad muscles because they'll seize up. I just need to get to flat ground." The rescuer calmed down, and informed us that the chopper was already on its way and to stay put. It was going to be a long-line rescue, since I could not see any place that even the best pilot could land.

Two hours later, every agency I could think of had arrived. There was the fire department, mountain rescue, sheriff's department, the military, and of course, an ambulance. The chopper had been circling for a while and came to the same conclusion I had: no place to land. I was put in a cage for the long line rescue, and strapped in. The only way to secure me was to place straps over my thighs, still covered in needles. The straps pushed the needles further in. I waited another twenty minutes strapped to a cage when it was announced that they had no one who was qualified to do the long-line rescue. I was getting upset. Worse, we were running out of water. All the rescuers had hiked out, and very few had brought water. It was still over 100 degrees and sunny. They were drinking all of our water. It was a sheriff's helicopter, and not the rescue helicopter, that finally found a spot to land, and I was carried to it. I was then transported to the first helicopter, which then flew me to the hospital.

I knew it was now going to get worse; it was time for all the spines to come out. The emergency room must not have dealt with cactus injuries often. The first thing they tried was tape. I tried over and over to tell them that the method of tape or glue wouldn't work with the two-inch barbed spines of the jumping cholla, especially when they were pressed a full inch into the skin and muscle. They proceeded with the tape anyway. The tape did remove one thing: most of the hair on my left leg. Finally, I was given morphine, and I believe later, ketamine. The last thing I remember was a new person covering my leg with glue.

I awoke to find the spines removed. The problem was my leg was still partially glued together, and what hair I had left was being pulled every time I bent my leg. They had started using tweezers, but the tweezers did not have enough grip to pull out the embedded spines, so they quickly switched to pliers. I called my roommate, and he came to pick me up. I was looking forward to some Vicodin and a nap. By the next day, I was covered from head to toe in red dots and large bruises. For a week, my muscles continued to cramp up whenever I tried to use them. After a couple weeks rest and some muscle relaxers, I eventually made a full recovery.

While my rescue did not go very smoothly, I was very grateful for everyone who helped. I could not have gotten off the mountain any other way. A special thanks to the military who helped carry me to the helicopter, and the pilot who braved the landing. I appreciate the nurses pulling out spines on me for over two hours, and dealing with me while I was on drugs. Of course, thanks to my supervisor and crew leader, who both handled the situation extremely well.

It was during the recovery of that injury that I started this book. I started thinking about life after the field, and if I could keep living the way I had been. At this point, I was starting to have doubts about my long-term future in field biology.

***

Before my cactus injury—and especially after—I was noticing

something about my crew and myself. More and more, I found myself getting winded while trying to keep up on hikes. I picked my paths more carefully, and took longer to hike up and down steep terrain. On especially hard days, I could still keep up and do my job, but it seemed that my younger coworkers always recovered quicker. They could rest an hour and be ready to go back out there.

I was only 32, but I was feeling old. My joints ached from previous injuries, especially my knee. I had dislocated it three times in my life, though never in the field. I did it twice while playing sports, and once while jumping a fence. Now, when hiking I could feel it in my knee. I wondered how many cactus spines had broken off under my patella and how that might affect me. My back hurt after a few days of hiking with a couple gallons of water and my field gear in my backpack. This had never happened before.

I know 32 is not very old, but I felt older. Maybe it was because I didn't take care of myself. I drank too many beers, and spent too many nights without enough sleep, only to get up and work a full day. I had had too many falls down steep terrain, and too many days hanging on the cusp of severe dehydration and heat exhaustion. I gained and dropped weight seasonally, and my diet was never very good. It all seemed to catch up with me at once, and while I could still keep up with the younger techs, it was only a matter of time when my value would be more in experience and guidance, rather than boots on the ground. I needed to take the next step in my career.

12 The Next Step

The life of a traveling field biologist has been good to me. It has been hard, but I wouldn't have had it any other way. I've met some amazing people, and have had unforgettable experiences. It hasn't been what I expected, but I wouldn't exchange the adventures I've had for anything else. Actually, I probably could have done without falling down the mountain of cactus, though in the end, it did inspire me to write this book.

While I will never truly leave the field of biology, I am headed down a different path, and I have begun taking steps to do my part for conservation in other ways. At this moment, I am planning to become a biology teacher. My hope is to inspire the next generation of conservationists and ecologists. I will still get out in the field on occasion—I love it too much not too—but it will mainly be for volunteer work and recreation.

***

The stories in this book are just a few of many. I have many more stories, and have heard even more from my coworkers over the years. No one person's journey is the same. Every biologist has had a different experience than I have had, but I think most biologists can relate in some way to the stories mentioned here.

I would like to give some final advice to anyone thinking of going into this line of work: it will be hard, you will know pain, you will not have a normal life, but your life will be filled with amazing sights, memories, and people that few other jobs can match.

For everyone else, take a few minutes and go to your local park or forest. Find a mountain or a wilderness area and just walk. You don't have to go far; just look at it and think of all that there is in there. Think of the mountain lions and the hawks. Think of the deer fawns, the turtles, and plants. Think of all the amazing creatures and sites that are out there. No amount of conservation will work if the people stop thinking about the wilderness and what lies beyond the cities.

Afterword: Thank You

I want to thank all the biologists that work at government offices all over the country, the office staff that could work at higher-paying jobs, but choose to help the non-profits and government agencies. I want to thank the game wardens and wildlife managers that help maintain the balance between hunting and conservation, and the fisheries biologists that keep the native fish going while providing good sport fishing for the public. I want to thank all the policy-makers that try to balance all interests while being pressured from all sides. Thank you to the interns and volunteers; even if it is not your career, your work is what helps conservation programs succeed. Thank you to all the people that make responsible and informed decisions while shopping. Sometimes, the biggest way to help is to support responsible, ethical companies. Thanks to the vegans and vegetarians that switched, not because they don't like meat, but to minimize their ecological footprint—you are all stronger than I am. Thank you to everyone that recycles, reduces, or reuses. Every little bit counts, so keep it up. For those of you who walk or ride a bike when you could easily drive, I thank you.

A big thanks goes to my editor, Mike Zerwekh, who spent countless hours correcting my spelling and punctuation, and listening to story ideas. Thanks, Mike! Thank you to all of my coworkers over the years; you all have taught me so much! I would also like to thank my teachers, from high school science to my biology classes at Arizona State; all of you helped inspire me and lead me here.

Finally, my biggest thank you goes to all the wildlife technicians out there. All of you work hard, often putting yourselves in potentially dangerous situations for little money. You do it because you care, love your job, and love nature. All of you are awesome. THANK YOU!

ABOUT THE AUTHOR

Scott Lillie has been a wildlife biologist for ten years. Though mostly working in the Southwest, he has also traveled all around the United States for conservation and research projects. He resides outside of Phoenix, Arizona, where he enjoys hiking, viewing wildlife, and spending time with friends and family.

43767688R00086

Made in the USA
Middletown, DE
18 May 2017